The Unhappy Medium

T0335327

The Unhappy Medium

SPIRITUALISM AND THE LIFE OF MARGARET FOX

by Earl Wesley Fornell

DRAWINGS BY LOWELL COLLINS

UNIVERSITY OF TEXAS PRESS · AUSTIN

Requests for permission to reproduce material from this work
should be sent to:
  Permissions
  University of Texas Press
  P.O. Box 7819
  Austin, TX 78713-7819
  http://utpress.utexas.edu/index.php/rp-form

Library of Congress Catalog Number 64-10317

ISBN 978-1-4773-0597-3, paperback
ISBN 978-1-4773-0598-0, library e-book
ISBN 978-1-4773-0599-7, individual e-book

TO MARTHA

PREFACE

The literature on spiritualism includes hundreds of books, journals, and periodicals, as well as annual reports of the several societies which once supported spiritualism or which, on the contrary, saw such a belief as an evil anti-Christ and hence devoted themselves to its annihilation.

Because of the bizarre character of spirit rapping and the tent-show characteristics surrounding many of the mediums the public press in general took a keen interest in the cults. Also, because some of the greatest editors in the nation on occasion appeared to entertain the possibility that beings from another world might actually be near at hand knocking upon mortal doors, editorials and news stories in the press attracted public interest and increased the fame of spiritualism.

For this reason old newspaper and periodical files constitute a major source of documentation illustrating the social impact of the phenomenon of spiritualism. It is significant that such general periodicals as *The Atlantic Monthly, The Dial,* the *Scientific American,* the *Nation,* and others often printed serious articles speculating as to the validity of the claims made by the spiritualists.

Individual mediums—some sincere believers, others irresponsible adventurers—wrote books detailing their strange experiences with immortal beings. Many of these volumes were accepted by believers as divinely inspired and were put forward as equal to the books of the Christian apostles. The catalog of any large research library will contain cards for many dozens of these volumes, as well as for dozens of other books written to denounce the claims of the spiritualists.

Since these remarkable claims had attracted the interest of an estimated twenty million Americans, the politicians, of necessity, had to include the spiritualists in their calculations. While the orthodox churches on the whole wanted the law to curtail the spiritualists, the number of Americans who took an interest in the spirits numbered as many as those attached to any single one of the older religious denominations. In these circumstances the legislators had to treat with proper respect memorials and petitions sent to them by the spiritualists. There was after all a spiritualist vote and members of these organizations were ardent memorialists and petition signers.

Thus, the researcher can frequently find in the *Congressional Record* and in the records of the state legislatures interesting references to spiritualism.

The reports, diaries, memoirs, and private papers, both in printed and manuscript form, of persons and groups living during the last half of the nineteenth century often reveal colorful bits about the cult. To mention but a few, the diary of George Templeton Strong, Horace Greeley's memoirs and papers, the correspondence of Margaret Fox and Elisha Kent Kane, Ralph Waldo Emerson's notes, Leah Underhill's notes, the letters of Harriet Beecher Stowe, the report of the famed Seybert Commission of the University of Pennsylvania, and the reports of the harassed medical society of Buffalo will illustrate the keen interest which the rapping spirits aroused on all levels of American society. Later, when the cult was discredited, it is likely that many persons purged their diaries and letter files of favorable comments about spiritualism.

As mediums were often brought before the courts of law upon one charge or another, the records of the law courts, mostly in the lower and unreported levels, contain many interesting details about the tribulations of the unorthodox spiritualists.

In addition, the schools and colleges were the arenas for many of the battles between orthodoxy and spiritualism. Thus, in the records and newspaper reports concerning institutions such as Harvard and the University of Pennsylvania, and from such great school systems as that of New York City, as well as the unpretentious meetings of country school boards in the middle west, one can find an occasional account of an investigation into the phenomenon of spiritualism. The issue usually turned upon the validity of the claims of spiritualists and upon whether or not a believing spiritualist was fit to be a teacher of the young.

The work I have attempted in this volume is intended only as a brief account of a few episodes arising out of the interesting flowering of a strange cult during the last half of the nineteenth century. An attempt to evaluate the influence of this cult upon the social and political history of the United States or its effect upon the fundamental religious faith of millions of Americans would be a research task of far larger proportions. And to attempt to evaluate the extrasensory aspects of the implications arising from a scientific approach to the supernatural cults is a matter much beyond the social and political historian. I have merely chosen to illuminate what appear to be representative episodes, as illustrations of what must have been the larger story of spiritualism in America.

ACKNOWLEDGMENTS

I wish to express my gratitude in particular to Dr. F. L. McDonald, president of Lamar State College of Technology and to Professor Lloyd Cherry, director of the Lamar Research Center, for their interest in and support of my research.

I extend my sincere thanks to my friends at Lamar State College of Technology, who have assisted me in many ways: Dr. Richard B. Setzer, vice-president and dean, Dr. Edwin S. Hayes, dean of arts and sciences, Dr. Irving Dawson, chairman of the Department of Government, Dr. Preston Williams, chairman of the Department of History, Dr. Charles Hagelman, chairman of the Department of English, and Dr. Claude Boren, chairman of the Department of Sociology, and to Miss Julia Plummer, librarian.

All researchers are in particular debt to librarians for their expert advice and assistance in matters of bibliography and editing of footnotes. In this instance, I give my most grateful thanks to Miss Maxine Johnston, reference librarian at Lamar State College of Technology, and to Dr. James W. Phillips, formerly of Rice University, now cataloguer and bibliographer, De Golyer Rare Book Room, Fondren Library, Southern Methodist University, Dallas, Texas.

An academic researcher also is always in debt to friends and colleagues who helped and encouraged him in many ways. For their interest in my work during the early stages of the research, I am therefore especially grateful to Professor Edward Hake Phillips, of Austin College at Sherman, Texas; the late Professor William B. Hesseltine, of the University of Wisconsin; Professors Hardin Craig, Jr., Floyd Seyward Lear, Chalmers Mac Hudspeth, and Katherine Fischer Drew, of Rice University; and Dr. Ronald Drew and Dr. Stanley Siegel, of the University of Houston.

I wish to express my appreciation to other friends for their interest in my work: Mr. John Tod Hamner, Mrs. Rosa Tod Hamner, Miss Mary Tod, and Mr. Jeff McKinney of Houston; Mr. Charles O'Halloran, librarian, and his gracious staff at the Rosenberg Library, of Galveston; Mr. Robert E. Baker, of Galveston; Mr. Lowell D. Collins, dean of the Houston Museum School of Art and illustrator of this book; the late Thomas G. Rice, of Galveston; Dr. Lamar Cecil, Jr., of Princeton University; Mrs. Lamar Cecil,

of Beaumont; Mr. William G. Childs, Miss Kira Kalichevsky, Dr. Manfred
Stevens, Dr. William R. Tucker, Dr. Ralph Wooster, Professor William
Breining, Dr. Francis E. Abernethy, Dr. Samuel Evans, Professor Robert
Madden, Professor Ruth Coffey, and Professor Naaman J. Woodland, of
Lamar State College of Technology; Professor James C. Malin, of the University of Kansas; Dr. Jane Malin, of the University of Houston; Betsy
Fuermann and George Fuermann, of *The Houston Post;* Maxine Mebane
and the architect, Mike Mebane, of Beaumont; Evelyn Reveley and Dr.
Hugh P. Reveley, of Kerrville; Miss Alice Green, librarian at Amarillo;
Miss Doris-Gale Crownover, of Amarillo; Jean Garnsey and Dr. Clarke
H. Garnsey, of Wichita, Kansas; and Miss Esther McDermand, of Beaumont.

I also am indebted to the University of Texas Library in Austin, Fondren
Library of Rice University, the New York Public Library at 42nd Street
and Fifth Avenue, University of Texas Medical Library in Galveston, Texas
Medical Center Library in Houston, and the San Antonio Public Library
for their services.

I am most grateful to Mrs. Alice H. Finckh, editor of *The American-
German Review* of the Carl Schurz Memorial Foundation of Philadelphia,
for her interest and encouragement in my Texas research at the time that I
was writing this book.

I also want to express my particular appreciation to Eithne Golden Sax
of the United Nations, and Ernest Sax, both of New York City, for their
enthusiasm and sincere interest, throughout the years, in all of my research.

And finally, I want to thank my wife, Martha, for her invaluable assistance in editing and typing the manuscript for this book.

CONTENTS

ILLUSTRATIONS (*following page 98*)

The Unhappy Medium

"That motley drama—oh, be sure
  It shall not be forgot!
With its Phantom chased for evermore,
  By a crowd that seize it not,
Through a circle that ever returneth in
  To the self-same spot,
And much of Madness, and more of Sin,
  And Horror the soul of the plot."

—EDGAR ALLAN POE

MORE THAN A century ago the flamboyant spiritualist medium Margaret Fox made her debut in New York, created a sensation, and at once captured the popular mind of America. The youthful medium fascinated and frightened the Western world by her strange ability to establish direct contact with spirits and the hereafter.

She was a childlike clairvoyant, this Margaret Fox—a young woman of medium stature and immaculate, porcelainlike facial features, a remarkably white skin, expressive black eyes, jet-colored hair, "a petite, delicately moulded form, and a regal carriage with an aristocratic air quite uncommon." By the middle of the decade of the 1850's she had acquired the poise of a seasoned stage performer. Her first notoriety had begun seven years before, when she was but a child of thirteen. With astonishing suddenness the contact which she established in 1848 with the spirits of the nether world not only raised Margaret Fox to a fame that approached the supernatural but also let loose a cult of modern spiritualism which, before it began to fade, boasted tens of thousands of followers, thousands of mediums, and a host of apparently profound dissertations and journals devoted to a further understanding of the earth-shaking revelations which had originated from "the Rochester Rappings" of Margaret and Katherine Fox.

These signals from across the bridge of death were but the beginning of a grand séance which for the next half century was to see persons returned from the dead walking upon the earth, mingling freely with mortal Americans. Ceremonies were performed which united in wedlock the living and dead; ghostly schoolboys returned from the land of the spirits to revisit their old schoolhouses, upsetting the dignity of earthly classrooms. In one remote Iowa city sewing machines of the local textile mills were said to be operated by the spirits during odd midnight hours fashioning raiment for their ghostly use. Drivers of owl horsecars in the rising cities of Michigan were intrigued by beautiful female spirits who rode their cars at night and promptly vanished if approached for a fare. These were but a few of the many bizarre incidents caused by the return of the spirits to America over a century ago. There were many others.

Grave legislators in the Congress at Washington having cognizance of these strange occurrences debated what action the government ought to take with regard to the matter of spiritualism, and even the wise and humorous Abraham Lincoln during the Civil War years occasionally took fleeting and light-hearted counsel from the spirit visitors as to the conduct of the war. The issue of the spirits also became a matter of profound contest in the courts of law, in the religious counsels, in the halls of the great universities as well as in the drawing rooms of the brahmins of Boston and across the seas among the intellectuals of Queen Victoria's glorious, mid-nineteenth-century England. By a strange and interesting coincidence, the renowned arctic explorer and national hero of the time, Dr. Elisha Kent Kane, became involved in the ill-fated world of Margaret Fox.

This fantastic spirit invasion, be it fact or fancy, delusion or a herald from "the Great Beyond," originated from the precocious being of a very young lady in Hydesville, New York, one February evening in the year 1848. Is it any wonder then that her fame spread around the world?

The stage and the scenery for the entrance of the young medium had already been arranged long before her family happened to rent a haunted house in Hydesville. Evangelical religion, New England shakerism, temperance crusades, abolitionism, utopianism, feminism, and mesmerism had become popular during the yeasty decades of Jacksonian democracy, and had generated dynamic social elements which afforded willing assistance to a revitalization of the age-old hope that some practical and demonstrable *rapprochement* could be made with the eternal world of the spirits. The compelling need for revival of the ancient doctrine of spiritualism found a means of expression in the phenomena of the Rochester spirits who chose to speak to this mortal world through the medium of two chosen vessels—the young Fox sisters, who fortuitously or perhaps by a grand design appeared in Hydesville in 1847.

Spirits in ancient and in medieval times had been akin to demons which often aroused dreadful fears. Their modern counterparts, such as those which were thought to be hovering about Hydesville, were of a friendly sort completely in accord with nineteenth-century progress and therefore eager to enable mortal man to step open-eyed across the threshold which heretofore had been shrouded in darkness, fear, and doubt.

The appearance of these emissaries from another world was particularly welcome, for the rise of science in the early decades of the nineteenth century had, to some extent, brought into question the validity of older religious dogmas. Such reform movements as Utopian socialism, temperance, abolitionism, and feminism arose from a demand for a better life on earth since science seemed to promise no after life.

Other attempts to meet this crisis were efforts to reconcile religion with the new scientific approach in such doctrines as Deism, Unitarianism, and Swedenborgianism. Some New England intellectuals discarded their old beliefs and developed the doctrine of Transcendentalism, which was a partial return to classical Platonism.

Still another endeavor was a frenzied search for positive and immediate proof of the immortality that science seemed then to set aside. One result of this effort was Millerite Millenialism, a movement begun by William Miller of Vermont during the second and third decades of the nineteenth century. After years of careful study of the scriptures Miller determined that the second coming of Christ would occur in the year 1843. Miller's impressive sincerity and the practical advantages of using such a conclusion as a means for arousing a great religious revival led such advocates of emotional gospel as the brilliant Reverend Joshua V. Himes, pastor of the Chardon Street Baptist Chapel in Boston, to promote Miller's cult into one which soon boasted many thousands of followers and dozens of giant tabernacles. Their newspaper, the *Midnight Cry,* and their clergymen agitated audiences with the question "Are you ready to meet your Saviour?" as the dreadful year of 1843 approached and eventually drew to a close. But when the years 1843 and 1844 passed uneventfully the efficacy of the Miller doctrine disappeared and its followers were forced to look elsewhere for a practical demonstration of immortality.

Mesmerism, a theory developed by an Austrian doctor named Friedrich Anton Mesmer, was another attempt during that period to find new solutions to eternal problems. This theory held that the stars, electricity, and magnetism combined to exert a profound influence upon human beings. In 1843 Andrew Jackson Davis, an American prophet of mesmerism, who soon became famous in upper New York as the "Poughkeepsie Seer," was employing self-induced mesmeric trances to diagnose and prescribe cures for various human ills. While in the throes of his spirit-trances Davis claimed to have had long conversations with Galen, the physician and writer of the Graeco-Roman world of the second century. He also testified to having met the ghost of Emanuel Swedenborg in a graveyard outside Poughkeepsie; this wraith urged Davis to assist in bringing to mankind a better understanding of Swedenborgian doctrines. In the early 1840's the Poughkeepsie Seer was gathering about him a considerable following and was publishing pamphlets explaining his psychic power under the general title of *The Great Harmonia.* Many persons believed that the Seer was pointing the way toward a practical spiritualistic liaison between the mortal and the eternal worlds.

Another American sect which claimed to be on the way to discovering a more direct contact with the next world during the early decades of the nineteenth century was the Millennial Church or the United Society of Believers—usually called the Shaker Society. This group, with colonies in upper New York state as well as in most of the New England states, was founded by Mother Ann Lee Stanley. Her followers advocated a return to a primitive faith and held the belief that God revealed his divine will to men while enthralling them in spasms of shaking, fits, and fervor. Devout converts claimed that during their fits, fainting spells, and trances they saw visions and received divine prophecy. Mother Ann received all of her inspiration and revelation while she was held fast by divinely induced trances which were essentially spiritualistic. Since she had been chosen by supreme powers to be the "Second Pillar of the Church of God" the revelations which the spirits imparted to Mother Ann were believed to be of great significance. Many persons expected that beings of another world were at any moment to make a demonstrable contact with mankind.

Such was the state of affairs on the eve of "the Rochester Rappings."

The Rochester Rappings

UPPER NEW YORK STATE was the region chosen by the spirits for their revelations because the people who lived there were willing to receive them and to accept their messages. Initiates in such matters were therefore not surprised in 1848 when a small frame house in Hydesville, near Rochester became the scene of some strange occurrences.[1]

The chosen instruments of the spirits were humble folk—a Methodist farmer, John Fox, his wife and their two little girls, Margaret, aged thirteen, and Katherine, aged twelve.[2] When Fox moved his family into the house in December, 1847, the dwelling was already haunted, or so it was said in 1851 by a Dr. J. B. Campbell who produced proof of his contention in the testimony of one Michael Weekman, whom the doctor had located and had persuaded with difficulty to tell his story.

[1] New York *Tribune*, August 20, 1849; Emma Hardinge, *Modern American Spiritualism: A Twenty Years' Record of Communication between Earth and the World of Spirits*, p. 29 (hereafter cited as Hardinge, *Modern American Spiritualism*).

[2] Philadelphia *Public Ledger*, May 16, 1850.

Weekman and his family had fled the house in 1847 as a result of a long series of strange and unnerving incidents which had begun soon after their arrival. Late one evening, so Weekman's recorded testimony ran, he heard a rapping on the outside door. He opened it expecting to find a caller, but to his surprise no one was there. This happened many times during the evening. According to Weekman, "he walked around the house several times trying to find the knocker, but in vain. Finally, he placed his hands and ear against the inside of the door, he sprung out and went around the house, but no one was in sight." Each time when the rapping was repeated he clearly felt a jar on the door. At last his family forced him to ignore the rappings for fear some harm would come to him from further investigations.[3]

Some weeks later Weekman's eight-year-old daughter, lying in bed shortly after the candle had been snuffed out, felt something like a hand pass over her bedclothing. When this "cold hand" touched her face and head the little girl became so frightened that she was unable to call out. Thereafter, she refused to re-enter the room at night. After enduring such experiences for eighteen months, the Weekman family fled from the house and from Hydesville.[4] Those cognizant of spirit matters later expressed the opinion that the spirits were testing the Weekman child to ascertain whether or not she was a suitable vessel, and maintained that her unresponsive behavior had no doubt offended the nocturnal visitors.[5]

Others reasoned that the molestation of the Weekmans had been expressly designed to vacate the house for Margaret and Katherine Fox. Whatever the explanation, it was obvious that the Fox family, and particularly the two little girls, had been reserved by unusual forces as instruments for communication with the mortal world. Mr. and Mrs. Fox were well known in the community. They were members of the local Methodist Episcopal Church and were acknowledged to possess characters unimpeachable for truth and veracity.

It was in February, 1848, two months after the Foxes had moved into

[3] *Ibid.*, June 10 and 11, 1850; for more detail see Ann Leah [Fox] Underhill, *The Missing Link in Modern Spiritualism*, pp. 5–19 (hereafter cited Underhill, *Missing Link*) and J. B. Campbell, M.D., *Spiritualism, passim.*

[4] Underhill, *Missing Link*, pp. 23 ff.

[5] Philadelphia *Public Ledger*, both June 10 and 11, 1850.

the house that noises began to disturb their rest during the night. At first, Mrs. Fox attributed the sounds to a shoemaker who lived nearby. But the shoemaker, when questioned, asserted that he had never mended shoes at night. When the sounds persisted, Mrs. Fox appealed to her son David who operated a farm some three miles from Hydesville and David thereupon spent several nights with his family. He heard the sounds but was unable to discover their source.

On one particularly memorable evening, Friday, March 31, the family retired early. Mrs. Fox had strictly charged the children to lie still in bed and take no notice whatever of the sounds; but as if to rebuke her the knocks became louder and more pertinacious than ever. The children kept exclaiming and sitting up in bed to listen to the sounds. Mr. Fox tried the doors and windows to make sure that they were locked, and every time he pushed against a shutter to test its security answering noises replied as if in mockery.

According to direct testimony taken shortly afterward, Margaret, the elder of the two Fox girls, lying snugly in her bed on that cold March night, protected by an armor of guileless innocence and accustomed by now to the invisible knocker, merrily snapped her fingers and exclaimed, "Here, Mr. Split-foot, do as I do!"

The reply was immediate. The invisible rapper responded by imitating the number of the girl's staccato responses. Now the child raised her thumb and forefinger in silent gestures of communication. And each time there was an appropriate reply. "Only look, Mother," cried the excited child, "it can see as well as hear!" [6]

This phrase was seized upon later by persons blessed with a knowledge of spirit matters as one of the most prophetic uttered in modern times. That it should have come from the lips of an innocent child was, in their view, quite appropriate, and they predicted that these eloquent bits would one day be engraved in monuments of bronze and marble and reverenced as holy writ.

The good Methodist woman, Mrs. Fox, caught in strange events and noting the childish irreverence of her daughters as well as the cowering

[6] New York *Tribune*, August 20, 1849; also see New York *Tribune* of December 5, 1849 as well as January 18, 19, 31, February 4, 19, March 6, 1850 for other similar reports.

fear of her husband, John, mustered the courage possessed by all mothers and herself addressed the invisible rapper. "Count ten," she commanded. And ten raps she heard. "How old is my daughter Margaret?" "How old is Kate?" "How many children have I?" All of these queries were answered correctly. After similar experiments the distraught mother cried out, "Are you a man that knocks?" To this there was no response, but when she put the next question, "Are you a spirit?" the response was an immediate rapping.

Then Mrs. Fox inquired whether the spirit would knock if she called in her neighbors. Receiving an affirmative response the good woman sent her quavering husband off to fetch a Mrs. Redfield who lived nearby. After this neighbor had arrived and been frightened out of her sleepiness by the responses to her several queries messengers were dispatched to other citizens of Hydesville. They also became involved, and far into the night these quaking mortals remained in communication with the spirits of another world.

Those who witnessed this strange occurrence and skeptics who later investigated it described it as the most weird and novel court of inquiry in the whole history of inquisitions. Some who saw a hopeful omen in the incident were most impressed by the fact that the awesome interrogations had taken place in a humble cottage bedroom in a remote and obscure hamlet before jurors of unsophisticated rustics and that the witness queried was a denizen of a world of whose very existence mankind had heretofore been ignorant. These country folk, in their innocence, had succeeded in breaking through "what had been deemed the dark and eternal seal of death to reveal the long hidden mysteries of the grave" and opened the portals to the world of the living dead. Hopeful persons pictured the very air as filled with the millions of the living dead. "Our city streets," they said, "are thronged with an unseen people who flit about us, jostling us in thick crowds, and in our silent chambers." Their piercing eyes scanned all mortal ways. "The universe is teeming with them; there are no dead; there is no death." This then was the portent of that memorable night at the Fox house.[7]

[7] Rochester *Democrat*, November 14, 16, 17, 20, 1848; also see P. T. Barnum, *The Humbugs of the World*, pp. 73–151.

All during the first week of April, a procession of neighbors came to the Fox house, some to laugh and ridicule, others in humble, fearful inquiry. At times there were as many as five hundred people who had gathered to hear the sounds, so great was the excitement. Most of the observers heard the rapping distinctly and many felt the bedstead jar when the sound was produced. Observers noted that the rapping was heard most distinctly near the large bedstead in the room and particularly so when Margaret was snuggled under the covers.

By various methods including a kind of rapping telegraph which enabled the rapper to impart more detailed replies it was established that the spirit was thirty-one years old; that he had been murdered a few years previously for his money; that during his mortal existence he had been married and had had five children; and that his wife was now also among the living dead. It was further ascertained that the spirit was that of an itinerant merchant-peddler who a few years previously had called to show his wares at the house now occupied by the Foxes. During the visit he had been murdered for the $500 which he carried on his person. Repeated efforts by the interrogators to secure the name of the murdered peddler failed. An attempt was made to identify Michael Weekman as the murderer, but the peddler kept insisting that the initials of his killer were "C. R." When it was also determined that the peddler's body had been buried in the cellar of the house, courageous men hastened below with shovels to exhume the evidence. In the darkness of the cellar they discovered much freshly loosened earth which, it was admitted, might have been dug up by rats. Although energetic digging uncovered no body, definite evidence of decomposed bones and signs of quicklime were said to have been found.

The interrogators were able to deduce that the peddler had been murdered on the Tuesday night when the hired girl Lucretia P. had been sent away, and the assailant had been alone in the house with the victim. Once the deed had been done and the money taken "the body was dragged through the parlor, into the butlery and thence down the cellar stairs and buried ten feet deep."

A further and deeper examination of the earth in the Fox cellar was said to have produced some bits of crockery, charcoal, quicklime, human hair, and a portion of a human skull according to the testimony of a local physician. By a process of elimination interested parties tried to fasten the murder upon Charles B. Rosana, a previous tenant of the fatal house, who by that time was living in Lyon, New York. The accused, hearing of this slander, produced a certificate of good character signed by forty-four persons. He insisted that he had been accused falsely by the spirits.

The remaining months of the year 1848 were most uneasy ones for the Fox family. Often, in the dead of night, Margaret and Katherine heard strange disturbances; furniture seemed to move, cold hands seemed to tug at the bed comforters, and one night in the darkness they heard a sound like a death struggle, a gurgling as of a throat, and a sound as if someone were dragging a body down the cellar stairs. Similar incidents continued to occur as well as occasional sounds of rapping.

Mrs. Fox, true to her ardent Methodism, sought the aid of clergymen of that faith in Hydesville and in Rochester. These godly men did not take a kindly view of the spirits haunting Mrs. Fox and her children; indeed, they severely censured her for such associations. Mrs. Fox insisted that she had prayed for months with all the fervor of true Methodism to be released from the power that tormented them and that all her prayers had been in vain. She pleaded with her religious advisors not to deny her the solace of Methodism in this crisis.

Since the house was continually thronged by curious inquirers, it was decided in July of 1848 that Margaret and Katherine should be sent to live with their older sister, Mrs. Leah Fish, who operated a music studio in Rochester. Less impressionable persons in Hydesville noted that the spirits never manifested their willingness to communicate except in the presence of the two girls.

Mrs. Fish presently began to lose her pupils because of the notoriety of her two sisters whom the spirits persisted in visiting. Eventually, Katherine was sent to stay in Auburn, New York. But fourteen-year old Margaret remained with Mrs. Fish and now the spirits grew even more persistent in communicating with her.

Many citizens of Rochester did not take kindly to the residence of

Margaret Fox and her spirits in the city, while strangers repeated atrocious slanders at her expense and accused the girl of being a willful impostor.[8]

At this critical juncture, a group of Rochester citizens who were friendly toward Margaret Fox and her family banded together, and shortly a "spirit circle" began to hold meetings with Margaret in the home of her sister, Mrs. Fish. Living in the house at the time was a bachelor, a Mr. Calvin Brown, who very much resented the introduction of Margaret and her friends in a household which had previously been tranquil. The resentment was returned and it appears that the spirits, or perhaps Margaret, sometimes threw books or other objects at Mr. Brown when he was so rash as to walk about the house at night.[9]

The spirit circle's gathering of evenings to witness the manifestations caused much unrest in the city and the clergy in particular lost no time in asserting publicly that Margaret Fox and her family were a "vile imposture and in league with the evil one."

Poor Mrs. Fox, shaken by her profound experiences and by the shocked reaction of many of the clergy in Rochester, prayed that the great bitterness might pass from them. She prayed thus many times during gatherings of the circle until at length the precocious Margaret, apparently moved by her mother's anguish, somehow managed to induce the spirits to rap out a farewell message, promising that they would harass their hosts no more. A "mournful silence then filled the apartment which had but a few moments before been tenanted with angels." The spirits had gone. One by one, the members of the now depressed circle separated and passed out into the silent moonlit streets of Rochester feeling as if some great light had suddenly gone out.

A fortnight passed and when inquiring callers learned that all was quiet their interest in Margaret Fox dwindled. But there were others —such odd clergymen of Rochester as the Reverends A. H. Jervis and Charles Hammond, and the Deacon Hale—who saw a very great loss

[8] Rochester *Democrat*, November 14, 16, 17, 20, 1848; see also Hardinge, *Modern American Spiritualism*, pp. 31–35 as well as D. M. Dewey, *History of the Strange Sounds or Rappings*, pp. 1–79.

[9] Hardinge, *Modern American Spiritualism*, p. 40.

in the disappearance of "the tender, loving and wonderful presence" of the rappings. And Leah Fish, now that her pupils had deserted her, seemed to be most regretful that the manifestations had ceased.

On the twelfth day of the great dearth, a special circle of the new devout collected in the Fox household around the vessel, Margaret. After an interval of silence one of the members inquired of the quiet air if the spirits would rap for them. To the unspeakable joy of all present they were greeted with a perfect shower of sounds.

The group now decided to stage a public lecture and a demonstration of spirit rapping in Corinthian Hall, the largest auditorium in the city. The program was to begin with a lecture narrating the history of the rappings to be followed by the appointment of a committee from the most respectable persons present in the audience to make an investigation of the rappings in a private session with the medium Margaret Fox. The results of this session were to be reported at another meeting. It was asserted that by this procedure both the advocates and the skeptics would be served and the truth of the matter established. There would, of course, be an admission charge of one dollar per person to cover the cost of the hall and other expenses. These non-spiritual details were left to Leah who had a talent for such things.

Some members of the spirit circle felt that the meetings should take place in a church and that the inquiry should be conducted by clergymen, but the spirits, on being consulted through Margaret, seemed to prefer a public hall. They were clearly willing to challenge public scrutiny and scientific investigation and promised to rap loud enough to be heard in a large public place. And so, on the evening of November 14, 1849, the first public rappings took place before a large audience. Mr. E. W. Capron, of Auburn, New York, delivered the address. The Reverend A. H. Jervis and other prominent Rochester citizens agreed to serve on the observing committee, some as friends and others as skeptics. As Mr. Capron spoke, the key passages of his address were punctuated by "distinctly audible, though muffled sounds of the raps." At the close of the meeting a committee of highly respectable citizens was appointed to investigate whether or not the thing was merely a humbug.

On the second night, before an eager and excited audience, members of the investigating committee told the gathering that Margaret had given them every opportunity to inquire into the matter and that the essence of their report had to be that sounds were heard, and that the committee had completely failed to discover any means by which the raps were produced.

The majority of the persons in the hall were not pleased with this result; they obviously desired the entire exposure of the rapping humbug. A new committee of investigators was appointed. It included Dr. H. H. Langworthy, a lawyer named Frederick Whittlesey, and several others, all selected because they were known to be the least likely to be favorable to the hypothesis of a spiritual origin for the sounds; and in order to avoid possible deception this second examination was conducted in lawyer Whittlesey's office.

Even though Margaret was subjected to "cold, severe and often sneering scrutiny" the secret behind the rappings remained hidden. Dr. Langworthy tested the possibility that she may have been employing ventriloquism by placing a stethoscope upon her chest to uncover any unusual exercise of the lungs.

A fascinated witness of this proceeding was the New York Supreme Court Justice John Worth Edmonds who happened to be visiting his friend Chancellor Whittlesey. From that time onward the justice became an ardent spiritualist. When he first heard the raps, wrote Judge Edmonds, the innocent character of Margaret Fox convinced him that the demonstration was not a fraud.

As I entered the room, [said Edmonds] she was seated at one side of the table; the rappings came with a hurried, cheerful sound on the floor where I sat. I had taken my seat at the opposite side of the table, and listened with the idea in my mind that she was doing it with her feet, or hands, or knee joints. Directly the sounds came on the table, and not on the floor, and where her hands could not reach. It was ventriloquism, I said to myself. I put my hands on the table directly over the sounds, and distinctly felt the vibration as if a hammer had struck it. It was machinery, I imagined, and then the sounds moved about the table, and the vibration followed my hands wherever I put them. I turned the table upside down, and examined it so carefully as to know that there was no machinery . . . At times rappings in answer to my questions came on the back of my chair when no one was behind me.

Judge Edmonds was convinced that he was witnessing an historic event; it was a voice from beyond the grave that was speaking to mankind, he told the committee. It was not a doleful sound from the tomb, but a voice from beyond bringing great tidings of joy.[10]

Eventually, this second committee returned to the gathering at Corinthian Hall and announced that sounds had been heard, and that a thorough investigation had conclusively shown them to be produced neither by machinery nor ventriloquism, though what the agent was, the committee was unable to determine.

The audience was now most indignant. A third group of interrogators was immediately chosen whose members were selected on the basis of their previous sneers and scoffing. One of these was Lewis Burtis who had dared the Fox crowd to put him on the committee; another was Mr. L. Kenyon who stated that if he could not find out the trick he would throw himself over Genessee Falls.

Not only Margaret but Leah, who at that time made no claim that she was a medium, was subjected to a third interrogation. Mr. Burtis and Mr. Kenyon finally admitted that Margaret was too subtle for them to discover her trick. A committee of ladies was then appointed to examine the girl's clothes and body in an effort to uncover the fraud, but this tactic also failed. Finally, Margaret was completely disrobed and her garments examined carefully with the same results. During this ordeal the distraught girl wept bitterly. Her sharp protests and lamentations were overheard by a Quaker lady of Rochester named Mrs. Amy Post, who pushed her way into the room where the investigation was being held and promptly put a stop to the proceedings. Curiously enough, once Margaret had regained her clothes and had become aware of the powerful shelter provided by Mrs. Post's strong personality a shower of raps sounded indignantly as Margaret and her protector left the room.

[10] See New York *Tribune* of both March 28 and July 6, 1859 for more or less the same story.

That evening the usual audience gathered at Corinthian Hall to hear the latest report. The members of the committee, however, were loath to present themselves before the excited crowd which, with no protest from the conservative clergy in the city, threatened to lynch the rappers and their advocates if the committee should again fail to uncover the fraud. Eventually, Leah Fish, Mrs. Post, her husband Isaac Post, and the Reverend A. H. Jervis agreed to accompany the now pale and shrinking Margaret to the platform. As they neared the front of the hall another Quaker named George Willetts joined the spirit group declaring that if the mob of ruffians should attempt to lynch the girl they would have to do so over his dead body.

Immediately after the committee members had made their report, which indicated that although they suspected trickery they were none the less unable to identify the source of the deceit, a citizen named Josiah Bissell proceeded to distribute torpedoes among the boys in the audience. Soon the hall was rocking with explosions and ribald jokes, all supposedly emanating from the spirits. Then a gentleman in the audience rose to insist that the rapping was made by means of leaden balls that were sewed into the hems of Margaret's skirts. At this point a Major Packard formed a committee of young men who marched up to the platform determined to examine Margaret's dress and thus uncover the deception. Fortunately, the police intervened at this juncture, closed the meeting, and escorted the Foxes home in order to forestall a more serious disturbance.[11]

While most of the noisy spectators at Corinthian Hall had not been awed by the rapping sounds a considerable minority believed that they had been in the presence of divine revelations. These persons quietly sought out the Fox family and their followers. Soon secret spirit circles were holding meetings in various private homes in the city. Care was taken to avoid the attention of persons who might again arouse the rabble in an attempt to clear the town of this devilish activity.

At a charge of one dollar per person at these secret meetings Leah

---

[11] Rochester *Democrat*, November 15, 1848; also see same paper for November 16, 17, 18, 1848, for follow-up stories; the same details may also be found in the Philadelphia *Public Ledger*, June 10, 11, 14, 1850, and the New York *Tribune*, December 5, 1849.

was able to manage the Fox family's financial affairs without hardship. To assist in maintaining a lively atmosphere at these secret gatherings Leah composed a musical work called the "Spirit Song" which became the hymn of "the New Jerusalem." The music and the words of this hymn had been transmitted directly from the spirit world by means of the rapping telegraph.[12]

Judge Edmonds, who was a frequent visitor at the circles, brought other well known people to marvel with him at these strange events. The president of Union College, a close friend of Edmonds, also became interested in spiritualism and soon members of the faculty of that institution came up to Rochester to attend the circles. Later, other learned men such as President James Mapes of the Mechanics Institute, Robert Hare, Professor of Chemistry at the University of Pennsylvania, Horace Greeley, and many others of like stature came to hear the spirits rap. The Fox sisters, with the aid of other scientific-minded mediums and followers, soon perfected their tapping telegraph sufficiently to permit occasional contacts with the departed spirits of such illustrious persons as Benjamin Franklin, Thomas Paine, William Shakespeare, Francis Bacon, and John C. Calhoun, to name but a few.[13]

The fame of the Fox sisters and their spirit telegraph rapidly spread across the United States and Europe. Within a few months mediums who claimed to be able to make contact with the spirits of departed loved ones and to transmit messages from the living dead appeared by the hundreds in all parts of the world. Clergymen of the more liberal religions began to desert their former denominations to join the ranks of the more remunerative cult of spiritualism. Horace Greeley, in an editorial comment on spiritualism in the *Tribune,* wrote,

We think it fair to add that we have been present when rappings were made on tables and chairs when it was as certain as human sight could make it that no person whatever was in contact with the article from which the sounds came. "Ah!" says the doubter, "you thought they proceeded from the table, because you expected them there!" Well, a little girl, less than two years old, who had never before paid any attention to this matter, was attracted to the vicinity of the table by the loudness of the rappings and stood

[12] Underhill, *Missing Link,* pp. 57–72.
[13] Hardinge, *Modern American Spiritualism,* pp. 70–141.

near it for some time, looking curiously first upon and then under the table. [These things, added Greeley] cannot be disposed of summarily.[14]

A few months previously Greeley had asked a trusted friend to go to Rochester as an observer of the new phenomena. This gentleman returned admitting that what he had witnessed was not explainable by the hypothesis of mere jugglery. He said that on the occasion of his visit with the Fox girls he took his seat at a table and asked a series of questions as to the ages of his children and relatives; all the answers were correct. Influential citizens of Rochester told him that there were so many spirits about the city that at times the spirits would reach under the table at dinner and grasp the foot of a favored one. Some of the leading citizens in Rochester were both frightened and elated over this strange turn of events.[15]

The interest in the new phenomena soon began to affect the professions in upper New York State. It was rumored that a learned judge consulted the spirits before he handed down his rulings and that reputable members of the medical profession sometimes consulted the dead in a search for prescriptions for the living. In order to halt this retrogression to the dark ages Dr. Austin Flint, the famed medical professor, writer of profound medical treatises, and editor of the *Buffalo Medical Journal,* organized a committee composed of himself and Professors Charles Alfred Lee and John Wilson Coventry of the medical college in Buffalo which was charged with the mission of determining whether or not the raps actually were emanating from the bodies of the two Fox girls.

After several days of consultations the three specialists issued a statement to the effect that, in their professional opinion, Margaret Fox produced the raps by means of a subtle manipulation of her knee joints. Leah Fish, with a sense of timing worthy of a later day, immediately accepted the challenge of the medical profession.

In due time a meeting was arranged in which the committee of doc-

[14] New York *Tribune,* March 6, 1850; for more of the same type of interpretation see the *Tribune* for January 23, 1851 and the *Rochester Magnet,* February 24, 1850.
[15] New York *Tribune,* January 23, 1851; for a more detailed account see Underhill, *Missing Link,* pp. 1–50.

tors held Margaret's legs for an hour in a soundless room in the interest of science and communications. Whenever the fingers of the doctors' hands clutching Margaret's legs and knees relaxed momentarily out of sheer fatigue, mild rappings were heard.

Later in the investigation when Margaret's feet were placed on cushions stuffed with shavings no sounds were heard. Leah protested, explaining that the reason no sounds were heard while Margaret was standing on sawdust cushions was because the "friendly spirits retired when they witnessed the harsh proceedings of the persecutors." Dr. Lee admitted that he heard two sounds while holding Margaret's knees and five other sounds while a colleague had the girl's limbs clasped firmly in his hands. At the conclusion of the day's investigation the doctors stated that, in their professional opinion, the famed Rochester rappings actually originated in the knee-joints of the Fox sisters. This conclusion was extensively reported in the Buffalo *Courier and Inquirer* and later analyzed in a learned article which appeared in the *Buffalo Medical Journal*.

In this instance, however, the professors were not allowed to have the last word. As the investigation broke up in the late afternoon a more friendly committee took over the inquiry. This jury, composed of Captain J. C. Rounds, Judge John Burroughs, and Dr. P. A. Gray held fast to Margaret's knees for several hours. Standing alongside and occasionally clutching a knee were such well known upstate New Yorkers as C. C. Bristol, M. M. Gibson, Stephen Dudley, L. Rumsey, and N. Rogers. With all these reliable persons clutching at Margaret's extremities it was certain, said an observer, that she could not have "clapped her joints" without exposure; and yet "all present could still clearly hear the sounds." At the conclusion of the evening Leah issued a statement to the *Courier and Inquirer* daring Professor Flint to present the conclusions of the second committee in his forthcoming report to the medical journal.[16]

Interested persons who had hoped that some definitive conclusions might come from this investigation were disappointed. Greeley, for

[16] See Buffalo *Courier and Inquirer*, March 13 and 14, 1850; also *Buffalo Commercial Advertizer*, March 14, 1851 and "Discovery of the Source of the Rochester Knockings," *Buffalo Medical Journal*, VI (March, 1851), 628–642.

instance, engaged in a correspondence with Dr. Charles A. Lee on the matter of spiritualism which the publisher later printed in the *Tribune*. The doctor told Greeley that the University of Buffalo had privately carried on extensive experiments in an effort to present an acceptable answer to the delusion which was then sweeping the state. In February of 1850 Dr. Lee, who was then teaching at Bowdoin College in Maine, received a request from the University at Buffalo to return and give a series of public lectures to counteract the delusion. In accord with this request Lee searched among his acquaintances and patients until he found a man who could make joint raps which surpassed those made by Margaret Fox. With this demonstrator as his assistant Doctor Lee made a tour of upper New York State in an effort to quash the delusion; but what was ludicrous, wrote the doctor "was that many in the audience who now for the first time witnessed something in the spirit-knocking line became converts to the doctrine and still refer to my exhibition as the strongest kind of demonstration in its support."

"I had thought before the lecture," he said, "that I and my good friend would, as soon as our medical lectures were over, take a pilgrimage down East, taking Boston in our route and blow spiritualism sky-high by our demonstrations. But seeing such fruits from my well-intended efforts, I abandoned my project, and begged my assistant to rap no more." [17]

[17] Letter to Horace Greeley from Dr. Charles Alfred Lee published in the New York *Tribune*, July 22, 1859. For additional related details see Gilbert Seldes, *The Stammering Century*, pp. 331–347; Horace Greeley, *Recollections of a Busy Life*, pp. 234–241; William Harlan Hale, *Horace Greeley: Voice of the People*, p. 94; William Robert Gordon, *Threefold Test of Modern Spiritualism*, pp. 19–80; Eliab Wilkinson Capron, *Modern Spiritualism: Its Facts and Fanaticisms, Its Consistencies and Contradictions*, pp. 29–40.

The Gotham Spirits

In June of 1849, P. T. Barnum arrived in Rochester to observe the Fox sisters. He at once saw the possibilities inherent in the new phenomena. Leah Fox Fish was quick to see the advantages of an association with Barnum. A bargain was struck and in a short time the Fox girls were exhibiting their strange powers at Barnum's Museum and elsewhere in New York City at an admission charge of two dollars.[1]

Sophisticated New Yorkers such as Judge John Worth Edmonds were well aware that charlatans and chicanery had already found their way into the new faith. They were aware, too, that Margaret and Katherine Fox had a flair for showmanship. But these observers were convinced that both of the Fox girls had gifts of perception which defied ready explanation, and that Margaret, in particular, was often able to read the minds of those who visited her exhibitions. Justice Edmonds claimed to see a divine hand at work. Others saw merely a curious power in Margaret which warranted careful watching. The

[1] P. T. Barnum, *The Humbugs of the World,* pp. 73–88.

majority of the people who attended the exhibitions regarded the rappings as humbug even though they were not prepared to explain how the noises were produced.[2]

Horace Greeley attended the exhibitions and also visited the Fox girls at their hotel on the corner of Broadway and Maiden Lane. Greeley told Leah that she ought to charge an admission fee of at least five dollars to keep the rabble out. Leah, however, favored a lower admission charge; she wished to interest the general public as well as the intellectuals and it was she who got the Broadway songstress, Mary Taylor, to popularize a song titled "The Rochester Knockings at Barnum's." Meanwhile, jokes about the spirits became popular at that time.[3]

During the first three months, the sessions, some of which took place in the Museum and some in Barnum's hotel, were held in large parlor-type rooms around a table big enough to accommodate about thirty seats. "Receptions" were held from ten to twelve in the morning and again from three to five in the afternoon and from eight to ten in the evening. Private "sittings" were arranged during off hours for larger fees. The demand for Margaret's time was of course particularly great. Many of the "sitters" were sympathetic and ready to believe. Others, especially clergymen and members of the legal fraternity, were bent on trapping the young medium. Leah and Mrs. Fox, however, kept Margaret aware of the fact that the gross receipts of even a dull day's business were usually more than a hundred dollars.

The literate and the knowledgeable felt that the remarkable gifts of the two Fox girls ought to be examined carefully in more dignified surroundings than those provided by Barnum's Museum and began inviting the girls for extended visits in their homes.

On one occasion, when the girls were the guests of the editor Rufus Griswold, such well known persons as George Bancroft, James Fenimore Cooper, William Cullen Bryant, George Ripley, General Lyman, Dr. Francis, Reverend Joseph Tuckerman, and Nathaniel P. Willis were present. And Willis reported that everyone was remarkably im-

[2] Thomas Colley Grattan, *Civilized America*, II, 369–372; for further details see Horace Greeley, *Recollections of a Busy Life*, pp. 234–241.

[3] New York *Tribune*, April 22, 1850.

pressed not so much by the spiritualistic manifestations as with the clairvoyant gifts and the remarkable skill displayed by Margaret Fox in anticipating or penetrating unspoken thoughts. A friend of Horace Greeley's wrote that it was generally conceded that Margaret was a remarkably shrewd observer of human nature and many an individual who thought he was applying severe tests was unwittingly furnishing her with the means of answering his questions.[4]

In April of 1850 Horace Greeley entertained the Fox sisters in his Turtle Bay home. Greeley had taken a lively interest in the young mediums long before they came to New York, and he had engaged correspondents to follow the early developments of the manifestations in Rochester and Auburn. Years later, when he wrote his *Recollections,* Greeley tended to attribute his enthusiasm for the Fox sisters' revelations to his wife's interest in establishing communication with the spirit of their young son Pickie, who had then but recently died; but the record indicates that Greeley's interest in spiritualism was not merely that of a husband bent on humoring his spouse.

While the girls were still upstate Greeley had been impressed by the fact that the respected Rochester publisher D. M. Dewey had affirmed the verity of the rappings and that the clear-sighted and entirely impartial clergyman, the Reverend C. Hammond, was most impressed by the clairvoyant talent of Margaret Fox. In the late spring of 1850 Greeley wrote that while some parts of the exhibitions appeared to be the work of deception or collusion other aspects of the demonstrations could not be explained on the basis of fraud or natural laws as they were then understood. The noises, he said, were being produced by some means as yet not satisfactorily explained. The rappings, he thought, were best explained as an exercise of clairvoyance or some kindred psychologic phenomenon on the part of the deceivers which had not yet been fathomed by the investigators.

On one occasion Greeley and his friends acknowledged that they "had seen some things which were contrary to the natural and physical laws as they are now known." A bit later his skepticism had been aroused and he pointed out that "some persons not so dead are doing

[4] New York *Tribune,* April 22, 1850 and the New York *Journal of Commerce,* April 22, 1850 both give more or less the same details.

that rapping"; but a few days after that the editor was again pondering whether or not there might have been more to the matter than the public was ready to admit.[5] Meanwhile, other New York papers were refusing to take a serious view of the rappings.

It was in this state of mind that Greeley invited the Fox sisters and their mother to be his house guests. He had never given any credence to their asserted contacts with the great, long-dead figures of the past, but he did admit that contact with those recently passed beyond might be possible and for this reason he humored his wife's hope of securing a response from Pickie.

The editor was annoyed by persons who followed the Foxes from Barnum's to his home. Greeley did not want to turn his house into a show place. He found the assertions of contacts with such ancients as Benjamin Franklin and the jugglers' tricks of moving tables about to be but a degradation of the inherent possibilities which lurked deep in the latent talent displayed by Margaret and Katherine Fox and he wanted to separate their clairvoyant talent from the trickery which Leah had attached to their affairs under the tutelage of the master of this art, the great Barnum.

The Horace Greeleys, then in their early forties, were living in their Turtle Bay home, but the house had never been quite the same after the death of their son Pickie. Mary and Horace speculated as to the immortality of the soul and whether or not Pickie's soul was now residing elsewhere.

It was this curiosity plus the intellectual and journalistic interest which Greeley already had in the Fox sisters that prompted his asking the mediums to be his house guests for an extended visit. Soon the Greeley home became the meeting place for clairvoyants, spiritualists, and their devotees.

Jenny Lind, who was appearing in New York under Barnum's management, was among the illustrious persons who came to Turtle Bay to listen to Margaret Fox discourse with the spirit world. Greeley related in his memoirs that on the occasion when Miss Lind came the company had scarcely seated themselves around the table when audible

[5] New York *Tribune*, April 22, 1850.

and abundant rapping commenced. The great singer heard the noises and felt the table jar, but she had no wish to attribute this stellar performance to a rival female in the room and particularly not to another who was both "very pretty and very young." In a piqued voice and in a "tone and manner of an indifferently bold archduchess" she challenged Greeley, "Take your hands from under the table!" After a moment the editor understood that the great Nightingale was accusing him of assisting Margaret. "I instantly clasped my hands over my head," wrote Greeley, "and kept them there until the sitting closed."[6]

The sitting with Miss Lind ended on a discordant note provided by the great soprano. At other private sessions, however, there had been occasions when Mrs. Greeley was sure she had been in contact with Pickie and at times even the editor was inclined to believe that Margaret Fox had drawn a message from beyond.

On other occasions when such friends as Bayard Taylor, Theodore Parker, Harriet Beecher Stowe, James Fenimore Cooper, John Bigelow, and George Bancroft visited Turtle Bay, Margaret held the gathering entranced all evening. Some of the guests on these occasions were willing to take Margaret's skill at face value, others were merely willing to sit still for hours around her table with an open mind and even the skeptics who had been in close proximity to Margaret's person and felt the sting of some of her answers to questions they had facetiously directed to long-dead friends, were reluctant to declare that the girl was a fraud. It was only those who had merely watched her work in a large public hall who seemed ready to state categorically that she was the perpetrator of a hoax.[7]

The need at the mid-century point to find a spiritual counterbalance to the growing tendency to acknowledge science as the measure of the universe was so great that even many skeptics were loath to thrust aside the possibility that the accepted mechanistic view might be an oversimplification. They dared not scoff absolutely at the new door upon which Margaret rapped so beguilingly. A few, such as the elder Henry

---

[6] Greeley, *Recollections,* pp. 234–244; for interesting comment relating to this incident, see Gilbert Seldes, *The Stammering Century,* pp. 335–337.

[7] Allan Nevins and Milton Halsey Thomas (eds.), *The Diary of George Templeton Strong,* II, 186–192, 197–198 (hereafter cited *Strong Diary*).

James, saw Margaret as but one phase of a "modern Diabolism" which had thrust its ugly features into view.[8]

A form of diabolism may have been at work. At least, the dynamic Leah Fish sensed the financial as well as the religious opportunities which were made available to her from the sensation offered by Margaret's demonstrations. Leah, being twenty-three years older than Margaret, was well qualified to dominate her simple, superstitious mother and her younger sisters. She had been the generating source behind the larger revelations emanating from Rochester. The dual prospect of financial gain and the excitement of creating a new cult fascinated Leah. She made the most of both by dominating the other members of her family through fear and coercion.

The illustrious Englishman Thomas Colley Grattan, for many years Her Majesty's consul for the state of Massachusetts, wrote that it was not only the low and ignorant who yearned for the new assurance that grew out of Margaret's tapping, but also men of "high attainments, unblemished character and considerable talent" were found among those who believed Margaret Fox to be a terminal point of a message center to another world.[9]

Another Englishman, Henry Spicer, Esquire, of London, travelled in America and visited Margaret in Rochester at the height of the spirit-rapping craze and later was an observer at Margaret's séances in New York City. He remarked with considerable awe that "a matter which seems fraught with powerful interest to the estimable and intelligent cannot easily be put aside with scorn." He had watched Margaret at work and he soon became convinced that the mystery was "not mechanical" in its origin; that "no human intelligence, however shrewd and penetrative—in no hitherto recognized law of physics" could have produced the results which Margaret was able to evoke.[10]

Horace Greeley, having great respect for the masters of the ancient world, maintained his skeptical view of the messages which other me-

[8] Henry James, "Modern Diabolism," *Atlantic Monthly*, XXXII (August, 1873), 219–224.

[9] Grattan, *Civilized America*, II, 369–372.

[10] Henry Spicer, *Sights and Sounds: The Mystery of the Day, Comprising an Entire History of American "Spirit" Manifestations*, p. 73; also quoted in Grattan, *Civilized America*, II, 372.

diums then practicing in New York claimed were words of wisdom coming directly from the spirits of the sages of the past. He commented that the wisdom of the ancients as it was being brought back by the mediums failed to equal the intellectual brilliance usually attributed to these wise men. Even Old Nick, it seemed, was receiving an unjust representation. "Judging from the specimens of Satan's forensic and conversational ability given in the books of Job 1. 11 and Matthew IV," said Greeley, "we are sure Old Nick, if he were really to set about inventing messages from our friends in the spirit world" would present his case with much more effectiveness than was being done by the mediums who now presumed to speak for him.[11]

At times, however, it seemed that the spirits really were in league with Old Nick. A clergyman-medium named John Rogers reported to a convention of the faith in 1852 a baffling dilemma. The reverend had established a line of communication with a spirit answering to the name of Tom Paine; after a few days of conversation this "being" had begun to utter "many insanities and immoralities," and had the effrontery to claim that he was God. The reverend solemnly informed the convention that much care must be taken to protect one's self from such frauds operating in the Great Beyond. A Reverend Mr. Fishbough reported that he also had had a hard time with the spirit of Tom Paine who had "buffeted the Reverend Fishbough about." The reverend said he had tried to induce Paine's spirit to show more piety and good behavior, but Paine's other-world self continued to be a "bad boy" and to call Fishbough bad names and "would not go away when told." [12]

At about the same time the youthful medium, Daniel D. Home, was arousing hilarious consternation in some New York drawing rooms which he visited in private table tipping séances. On one occasion, said a witness, two persons sat on an ordinary table. In a few moments this piece of furniture "was agitated, then turned partly around, raised on two legs on one side, where it remained for a minute in plain sight of all; then raised in like manner on the other two legs, and so continued for some time, and finally it was rocked back and forth like a cradle."

[11] New York *Tribune,* February 23, 1853.
[12] *Ibid.,* December 24, 1852.

What really went on here, wrote one of Greeley's journalists who witnessed the scene, he would not venture to say, but he had seen it all in "clear gas light"; be it "trick, jugglery, magnetism, or spirits" he was at a loss to determine.

On another interesting evening in January, 1852, Charles Partridge and his wife, Dr. Oliver Wellington and his wife, Juddson Hutcheson, and the Fox sisters held a séance at Dr. Wellington's home. The whole party went into a large, dark closet and held hands in a circle as they had been directed to do by the spirits earlier in the evening. Soon the persons in the closet were touched by what seemed to be human hands. Some were natural and warm; others appeared cold, clammy, and deathlike. Charles Partridge related to Horace Greeley that "their size, temperature, and strength were clearly distinguishable." Some of the hands, Partridge went on to say, "appeared large and heavy like those of strong men grasping our arms firmly and forcing us from one side of the closet to the other and moving us with ease. Others appeared smaller and more gentle in their touch, while others appeared like the soft hands of children patting us upon the head and face. These touches were all over us from head to foot, simultaneously upon us or nearly so." This remarkable situation continued for two hours. One of the ladies refused to believe "the evidences of her own senses, and could not realize that the wonderful things we were experiencing could be produced by the spirits of our departed friends." Her lack of faith apparently irritated one of the spirits, said Partridge, for "her cap was suddenly taken off her head and placed upon the head of another person. Her comb was taken out and quickly put into my hair where it remained . . . and a large bass viol standing in the corner" was swung around against her and "the strings played by unseen fingers." [13]

There were many spiritualists, however, who deplored the buffoonery practiced by some of the spectral visitors. The Reverend Professor H. Mattison of the John Street Methodist Episcopal Church gave a series of lectures at Broadway Tabernacle in January, 1852, which, he declared presented Methodism's explanation of buffoonery among the spirits.

[13] All of the foregoing is based on a long letter written by Charles Partridge to Horace Greeley, printed in the New York *Tribune,* January 17, 1852.

There were, he said, good and evil spirits. The good spirits, he insisted, were entirely innocent of the undignified pranks charged to them.[14]

At Hope Chapel in Manhattan on Friday, March 5, 1852, the Reverend Samuel Byron Brittan delivered a lecture upon the "spirit crisis" which promised to enlighten even the most discerning intellects. This discourse was attended by a large and "deeply interested assemblage, among whom were noticed many of New York's most respectable citizens." The Reverend Mr. Brittan pointed out that the issue of spirit rapping presented a matter which had to be "faced up to" by men of intellect. Human beings, he said, occupied a threefold sphere of existence—sensation, reason, and intuition. Many persons never reached beyond the level of sensation. Many persons had no ideas beyond the impressions made by organs of the senses. They lived entirely in the province of the material. Men often classified themselves in the plane of sensation by their own confession. "We often hear it said by numerous persons," continued the reverend, "that they will believe only what they have seen with their own eyes or heard with their own ears. There is a higher sphere—reason, base of the sciences. A still higher sphere is that of intuition, by which we have cognizance of spiritual realities." It was on this level that the new developments now facing intelligent men must be met.[15]

While intellectuals as well as others in Gotham continued to probe the new mystery and to cross the palms of their favorite mediums who were now fast multiplying in number, a similar situation was developing in London. The famed British scientist Michael Faraday of the Royal Institution watched the rise of the new phenomena with growing alarm. Finally, in 1853, after reading various accounts of table tipping and rapping in the American and London newspapers which attributed the antics of the mediums' acrobatic furniture to new discoveries in electromagnetism, the good professor could stand no more. He wrote a blistering essay-long letter on the subject to the *Times* of London, a letter which was widely reprinted in America. He ridiculed me-

[14] New York *Tribune,* January 11, 1853.
[15] New York *Tribune,* March 8, 1852; for a related story see Robert Dale Owen, "How I Came to Study Spiritual Phenomena," *Atlantic Monthly,* XXXIV (November, 1874), 581.

diums, clergymen, and college professors who associated spiritualism with electricity in phrases which revealed that they "know nothing about the laws of these forces"; they speak, he said, as if "the earth revolved around the leg of a table"; he feared very much the result of "this mass ignorance" attempting to speak concerning matters about which it knew nothing. Employing several hundred words, Faraday explained why the claims of the mediums had to be fraudulent if looked at from a scientific point of view, and he closed with an apology. "I am a little ashamed," he confessed, "of having to write such an essay, for I think in this present age and in this part of the world it ought not to have been required."[16]

It was clear that Professor Faraday was not cognizant of the extent of the revolution being wrought by the invasion of the spirits. His parochial point of view might have been broadened if he had attended "The Great Bible Convention" held in New York June 3rd, 4th, and 5th in 1853, at which speakers asserted that the "very existence of the Hebrew law-giver was a myth; the creation a counterfeit; the Deluge a fable; the Exodus a forgery." Reason, said an unfriendly observer at the convention, had been displaced by mesmerism, clairvoyance and table rapping.[17]

With the negation of the Ten Commandments and other ancient laws, some members of the Spirit Faith began to develop new freedoms which were granted to favored members of a particular circle—a loosely organized band of believers who adhered to "Free-Spirit-Love doctrines," a concept asserting that "each man or woman has a natural, justly undeniable right to dissolve his or her existing sexual relation to a person of the other sex, if such he or she shall at any time have contracted, and entered into a new relation under the guidance of spiritual affinities or attractions." This group of men and women, who maintained a clubhouse cathedral in New York City at Number 555 Broadway, from 1853 to 1861, consulted the spirits in all matters of sexual mating. The congregation had a membership of over six hundred persons and held two evening meetings per week. Editors, who had sharp eyes

[16] New York *Tribune,* July 14, 1852; for a follow-up story on Faraday's letter see New York *Tribune* for July 15, 1852.

[17] New York *Times,* June 3, 1853.

for such societies, kept constant journalistic watch at the doors of this interesting organization. These Spirit-Love cults were seen as a peril to the city.[18]

Henry Raymond of the *Times* and E. Littell of the journal *Living Age* were much disturbed. They put the blame for the origin of this cult upon the "loose" theories advocated by Horace Greeley and his friends. "The seeds of this libertine philosophy," they said, "were first sown broadcast by the poems of Byron and Shelley and in the romances of Bulwer, George Sand, and Eugene Sue." [19] Later it was Robert Owen, Fanny Wright, Albert Brisbane, Margaret Fuller, and Horace Greeley, with their fostering of Fourierism in the United States, which had cultivated the immoral seed of sexual promiscuity which was now blooming at Number 555 Broadway. Thousands were fascinated, said Raymond, by Fourierism which they read about in Greeley's *Tribune,*

by its promises of a life of comparative ease, of social enjoyment, attractive industry, of relief from the burdens and restraints of family life . . . by the doctrine of passional attraction . . . which renders marriage as a fixed, sacred and permanent relation between individuals utterly impossible.[20]

Raymond asserted that Greeley, Brisbane, Margaret Fuller, and their friends, whether knowingly or not, had made possible the joining of the new religion of spiritualism with the antisocial doctrines of Fourierism and out of this unholy marriage of ideas the "Spirit-Free-Love System" had been given the sanction of a religion which would now dangerously increase its threat to society. Free-Love by itself, said Raymond, presented no threat to society, but harnessed in tandem with the spirits it became a diabolical chariot. Love Spiritualists were emigrating as far west as Minnesota. Their ideas, said the editor, seemed to have a particular appeal to the minds of Western people. "Clergymen, formerly preachers of evangelical denominations," he wrote, "are now lecturing

[18] New York *Tribune,* October 16, 1855; for a further story on spiritualism and free love see "The Free Love System," *Littell's Living Age,* 2nd Series, X (September, 1855), 815–821.

[19] "The Free Love System," *Littell's Living Age,* 2nd Series, X (September, 1855), 815–821.

[20] See New York *Tribune,* October 16, 1855, and also the New York *Tribune,* October 20, 22, 24, 1855.

on Spiritualism and its wildest heresies to large congregations. The whole West, and to a greater extent the whole country, has been deeply infiltrated"; and Horace Greeley, said the editor of the *Times,* must share the blame for providing a fertile soil for this new and poisonous weed.

Raymond appeared to be in a little awe of the phenomena of spiritualism. He was not at all certain that the rappings were all "humbug"; but what most horrified him was the meteoric rise of the new faith before reasonable men could ascertain its validity.

The rapidity [he wrote] with which this new faith has been extended is most remarkable. Its influence is wider, stronger and deeper than that of any philosophical or socialistic theory, since it appeals to the marvellous in man, and takes hold directly upon the strongest sentiments of his nature. Judging from its rapid extension and widespread effects, it seems to be the new Mohammed, or the social Antichrist, overrunning the world. In five years it has spread like wild-fire over this Continent, so that there is scarcely a village without its mediums and its miracles. It has its preachers, its public lecturers, its speaking and healing mediums, as well as those for test manifestations, its newspapers and its literature. It takes the form of a Church organization and has its religious services,—its prayers and hymns, its sermons and conference meetings,—at which its doctrines are inculcated and the personal experience of its adherents is set forth. If it be a delusion, it has misled very many of the intelligent as well as the ignorant. If a deception, it has deceived sharp intellects or made them its accomplices. If it be a diabolical enchantment, it surpasses in the extent of its influence any that the world has hitherto experienced. But whatever it may be, its direct hostility to Christianity, to its principles and its institutions, is manifest and palpable; and it has, beyond all doubt, exerted a very powerful influence to prepare the minds of its adherents for a ready acceptance of the belief that Marriage, as a legal and Christian institution, is at war with the doctrine of *spiritual* affinities, and to be treated accordingly.

Raymond went on to indict Greeley and his friends for paving the way for the new libertine doctrine of Spirit-Love. The article was widely read and reprinted in various monthly journals.[21]

---

[21] New York *Times,* October 16, 1855; see also the same paper for the dates October 20, 22, 24, 1855 for similar stories and attacks upon Greeley.

Greeley was jolted by the impact of the *Times* attack. He immediately disassociated himself from Spirit-Love and declared his loyalty to Christian marriage and the American home. These new libertine ideas, he said, were "bad—diabolically bad." The Spirit-Love doctrine, he asserted, was "unalloyed selfishness . . . It ignores the Divine purpose of conjugal union—children. Free-Lovers seldom have children, and still more rarely desire them . . . The woman who has changed her paramour repeatedly, and is likely to change again and again" was not fit to be a mother.[22]

In order to prove that he was no libertine the *Tribune* editor in October of 1855 launched a personal but "distasteful" investigation into the behavior of the cult at Number 555 Broadway. A female member of the club informed Greeley that their association was not wanton; she pointed out that whenever any "sensualists" who had somehow secured a membership made overtures to the ladies "unwarranted by passional spirit attraction," they generally received a severe rebuke from the ladies themselves, and were informed that they had mistaken the character of the place.

This reassurance failed to calm the editor of the *Tribune*. "How do these 'ladies'," he inquired, "know that the overtures are unwarranted by passional spiritual attractions?" How could the ladies determine that "their too eager suitors were not libertines?"

Members of the Spirit-Love Society, angered by Greeley's insinuations, asserted that not libertines but "Catholics, Evangelical Protestants, and great numbers of Unitarians and Universalists" constituted their membership. This defense, countered Greeley, was an insult to these religions as well as to the cause of honest spiritualists. "There is not a Christian Church," he said, "of any name or nature in this city which would not expel any member known to belong to this club." The Spirit-Love cults, he said, were a grave threat to family life, but their rise ought not to be blamed upon those who have previously spoken kindly of Fourierism, but rather the blame ought to be upon such men as Stephen Pearl Andrews and their campaigns against "Compulsory Mo-

[22] New York *Tribune*, October 17, 1855.

rality." It was clear, said Greeley, that the situation at Number 555 Broadway was a matter demanding action by the city authorities.

Aroused by Greeley's *Tribune* and some of New York's clergy, Police Captains John Turnbull and Abraham Kissner, and City Councilman Thomas B. Ridder raided the quarters of the Spirit-Free-Love Society; Benjamin Henderson, Henry Clapp, Jr., and the famous Stephen Pearl Andrews were brought before Judge Henry Osborn's court, in the city, to answer the charges against the society for advocating free love. The police had made arrests on the basis of Greeley's exposé rather than on actual evidence found upon visiting the rooms of the society. Judge Osborn was most critical of this procedure and he threw the case out of court after the following observation:

If the meetings held twice a week at that place are in contravention of the law; if individuals commit any unlawful act either there or elsewhere, let them be dealt with as the law directs; but the peaceable assemblage of two or three hundred for conversation, dancing, and kindred recreations is not a legal offense, and the police are not justified in arbitrarily suppressing it. Such is the law here and elsewhere and as such it henceforth must be respected and obeyed.[28]

Fortunately for the comfort of the orthodox in the city, the Spirit-Love cults were chastened by the furore they had raised and thereafter exercised a commendable caution in limiting the extent of their public display or the proselyting for their faith. Their only known exuberance occurred when they staged occasional "pic-nics" and steamboat parties up the Hudson River. These affairs were most interesting excursions indeed.

During the first few years of the 1850's while the spiritualist sensation was attracting wide interest in New York and elsewhere, the Fox family

[28] New York *Tribune,* October 20, 1855; see also New York *Tribune,* October 22, 24, 1855. The record of *Spirit-Love Society* v. *City of New York,* Unreported Cases of Judge Henry Osborn's Court for October, 1855, is to be found in Foley Square Court House files, New York City, New York. We may note that the engraving of a scene in Broadway in 1855 which is reproduced in this volume shows the address of the headquarters of the Spirit-Free-Love Society as 553 rather than 555.

was earning a lush living by holding table sittings in private homes in the city and in parlor rooms of hotels. Margaret Fox, the original fountainhead of the new faith, always commanded large and respectful audiences. As the size of these audiences indicated to Leah the monetary possibilities of spiritualism she decided to send Margaret and her mother on a tour of Philadelphia and Washington in response to the many invitations they had received. Leah, by that time having established herself as an important medium in her own right, remained in New York to keep the spiritual fires burning while Margaret was taken upon missionary journeys. According to Margaret's own account invitations to visit the principal cities poured in upon the family, "sometimes a half-a-dozen telegraphic dispatches" in a single day.

When the Greeleys were informed of the planned journeys they aroused a storm. The editor pointed out that Margaret and Katherine, the two initiators of this new speculation in science and spirits, ought, in the interest of common logic, to be given a good education. Although Greeley deplored the excesses of the spiritualists he was not yet ready to abandon the possibility that the Fox sisters might be the source of a great human discovery. Because he wanted to see their minds developed he offered to educate the girls if they would remain in the city. Leah and Mrs. Fox agreed to spare Katie if the editor wished to give her an education, but Margaret, the touchstone of the enterprise, would have to accompany her mother to Philadelphia. Thus it happened that in the autumn of the year 1852 Margaret began holding sessions in the bridal suite of rooms at Webb's Union Hotel on Arch Street in the City of Brotherly Love.

Margaret's exhibitions created a sensation in Philadelphia. The most "prominent and fashionable people of the city came to hear the mysterious knockings and to have their questions answered. Clergymen and doctors, scientific and literary persons, the lovely and the learned, the sentimental and the stern, were daily in attendance; and yet the wonder grew."

Among the "lovely" who came were female members of the illustrious Pennsylvania family of which Judge John K. Kane was a senior member. It was in these circumstances that the famous young naval surgeon and Arctic explorer, Doctor Elisha Kent Kane, was induced to visit the "bridal parlors" at the Union Hotel to hear Margaret Fox talk with the spirits.[24]

[24] [Margaret Fox] *Memoir and the Love-Life of Doctor Kane: Containing the Correspondence and a History of the Acquaintance, Engagement and Secret Marriage between Elisha K. Kane and Margaret Fox,* pp. 22–26; hereafter cited as Fox, *Memoir.* All letters cited between Elisha K. Kane and Margaret Fox are from the collection printed in this volume unless otherwise indicated. This collection is not always trustworthy and must be used with caution.

The Medium and the Explorer

IT WAS IN the late autumn of 1852 that Elisha Kent Kane first saw Margaret Fox. Margaret, under the management of her mother, was then holding manifestation sessions in the bridal suite at the Union Hotel in Philadelphia. The sessions were a sensation, particularly among educated people, and one morning at about ten o'clock Dr. Kane and several of his friends came to see the famous medium.

As Kane came in, Margaret was sitting beside a window of the large parlor studying her French lesson. Noting the domestic aspect of the scene, Kane decided that he had stumbled into the wrong suite of rooms; but when he inquired he was told by Mrs. Fox that he was indeed in the presence of the celebrated young medium.

The parlor gradually filled with visitors, but Margaret continued to study until she was summoned by her mother to begin the demonstration. While it went on, Kane sat with Mrs. Fox, a little apart. One of the young medium's friends described the meeting a few years later.

Little as she [Margaret] suspected his feelings, he loved her at first sight. Her beauty was of that delicate kind which grows on the heart, rather than captivates the sense at a glance; she possessed in a high degree that retiring modesty which shuns rather than seeks admiration. The position in which she was placed imposed on her unusual reserve and self-control . . . To appreciate her real superiority, her age and the circumstances must be considered. She was yet a little child—untutored, except in the elements of instruction to be gained in country district schools, when it was discovered that she possessed a mysterious power, for which no science or theory could account. This brought her at once into notoriety, and gathered around her those who had a fancy for the supernatural, and who loved to excite the wonder of strangers. Most little girls would have been spoiled by that kind of attention . . .[1]

In the weeks that followed Kane and his friends paid many visits to the suite at the Union Hotel. The explorer said later that from the very beginning he had been struck by Margaret's retiring modesty and her superior aloofness from her audience. The self-control and unusual reserve which she imposed upon herself when she was engaged as a medium conveying messages across "the Great Divide" made a profound impression upon Kane. Margaret's answers, he said, revealed a natural beauty and charm composed of a rare delicacy, simplicity, and firmness of character which held his attention despite the fact that he put no credence in the young medium's claims to be in communication with another world.

On one occasion Kane followed Margaret away from the table and said bluntly, "This is no life for you." He went on to point out the dangers of being so continually on display. "You ought to be in school," he said, "and remain there until your education is completed." Margaret admitted that she found no particular pleasure in her profession and indicated to Kane that it was her timidity that kept her close to her older sister and her mother. Then, on a December morning Kane sent Margaret a note. The day was so beautiful, he wrote, that he felt tempted to go for an early drive and asked her to accompany him. She agreed. It was some time later that he went so far as to inquire whether

[1] Fox, *Memoir*, pp. 24–26.

or not "she had ever been in love." To which Margaret replied with the plaintive answer that he could "ask the spirits."

Now Margaret or her mother began to receive a note almost every day. Some of them ran as follows. On December 7 he wrote to Mrs. Fox,

Dr. Kane will call at three o'clock p.m., for the purpose of accompanying Mrs. and Miss Fox upon an afternoon drive.

On December 10 he wrote directly to Margaret,

Dr. Kane leaves for New York on Monday; might he ask Miss Fox at what hour she would be disengaged before his departure?

On the 18th he wrote rather more at length to Mrs. Fox,

My dear Madam—I left New York this morning, and return again to-morrow . . .

I will call between five and six o'clock this afternoon.

I could not resist the temptation of sending the accompanying little trifle of ermine, for Miss Margaretta's throat. As I know you to be carefully fastidious as to forms, permit me to place it in your hands.

Pray pardon the pocket-worn condition of the enclosed note.

Very faithfully your ob't serv't,

E. K. Kane.

By January, 1853, Kane had established friendship not only with Margaret but also with Mrs. Fox. His favorite cousin, Mrs. H. J. Patterson, often had a vacant place in her carriage on sunny afternoons and on these occasions the young medium and the doctor accompanied his cousin on extended drives about the city. Margaret was notably happy on these excursions. She had a very charming way of expressing her delight at the passing scene; her reaction was "sparkling and irrepressible, yet marked by a modesty that was almost a timidity" which seemed to ask if the joy might be indulged.

She had learned self-command from being frequently in the presence of persons uncongenial to her, and from the blending of this habit of reticence with a natural gaiety which almost defied restraint. Her singular environment, as Doctor Kane once expressed it, made Margaret Fox a curious study; and on a particular Sunday morning late in January of that year Margaret expressed the same idea when she wrote "Now, Doctor—be candid!—am I not correct in saying that you are an enigma past finding out? You know I am." [2]

With increasing concern Kane persisted in anxiously reminding Margaret of the melancholy way in which she was living; he deplored the deceit which he knew must accompany her activities and which she tacitly admitted. He reminded her that she was "fitted by nature for better things," that she would, if she persisted in following the life of a medium, deny herself "the highest destiny of woman." Finally, he asked her earnestly if she would consider quitting her present life at the medium's table, devote herself to acquiring an education, and eventually entertain the idea of becoming the wife of Dr. Kane.[3]

Margaret answered that she could consider such a suggestion, but it was clear that her enthusiasm at this prospect was somewhat less than his. Kane, in an ungallant moment, pettishly told her that his family would most certainly disapprove such a matrimonial alliance but that eventually her charm and remarkable natural talents would overcome this familial objection.

When Margaret told her mother of Kane's remarks Mrs. Fox said that Leah would never allow such a thing, and anyway, the explorer was already committed to embark upon a second arctic voyage, to rescue Sir John Franklin. The probability was that Margaret's prospective husband would never return from this hazardous enterprise. Since the sessions provided the family with a livelihood, Mrs. Fox told Margaret that she could not quit the table to go off to school to prepare for a marriage that might never come to pass.

The doctor often discussed Margaret's situation with Mrs. Fox. He told her of the "duty before him to search for Sir John Franklin, the impossibility of marriage before his return," and that Margaret ought to complete her education before such an event could take place. "She must be fitted to occupy a high position in society" he would say as he

---

[2] *Ibid.*, pp. 27–31, 46.

[3] Quotations found in New York *Herald*, October 21, 1888; for more related material see Davenport, *The Death-Blow to Spiritualism: Being the True Story of the Fox Sisters As Revealed by the Authority of Margaret Fox Kane and Katherine Fox Jencken*, pp. 209–213. Hereafter cited Davenport, *Death-Blow*.

brought "books, and music, and flowers—the richest and rarest—several times a day." Once, presenting her with a camellia, he said "Like you, it must not be breathed upon." His attentions by this time—with all his precautions—could not fail to be noticed in Philadelphia. This embarrassed Kane because he was not prepared to acknowledge publicly that he had become fascinated by the teen-age spiritualist. Sometimes he sent his brother to the hotel in order to exchange letters with Margaret. In one instance Kane wrote Margaret, "I was unwilling to call upon you tonight for fear of talk; but I told my brother if you had company to show my ring, so as to avoid the mention of names. Do not let him suppose you have anything more than spirit business with me." [4]

A few days later Kane, having gone to New York on arctic business, wrote to Margaret telling her that he was most disturbed because the New York *Herald* that day had printed a story of a suicide in which Leah's name was mentioned. Apparently, some unfortunate soul had decided to end it all as the result of a talk with the spirits under Leah's dubious mediumship.

[4] Fox, *Memoir*, p. 43.

"Oh, how much I wish," Kane wrote Margaret, "that you could quit this life of dreary sameness and suspected deceit." Margaret suggested that he forego his quixotic arctic venture and perhaps they both could look forward to a more regular life. She accused him of being an enigma. That was all nonsense, he replied, "you understand me very well. I have my sad vanities to pursue. I am as devoted to my calling as you, poor child, can be to yours." He accused her of trying to manage him. He admitted that he was caught in the dilemma of a thirst for the grim duty of his arctic undertaking and a fascination for "the gilded dust of a butterfly's wing; and [I am] a fool because, while thus caught, I smear my fingers with perishable color." If nothing more came of their having met, he wrote, perhaps the memory of the incidents when they had enjoyed each other's association could be recalled "as a sort of dream, that Doctor Kane of the Arctic seas loved Maggie Fox of the spirit rappings." [5]

Near the end of January 1853 Mrs. Fox and Margaret returned to New York where they set up a new spiritual establishment on Twenty-Sixth Street. Margaret was relieved of some of the burden of table sitting by an older person who was also a medium. By that time it was possible to secure the services of other persons with spiritualistic talents who could demonstrate at manifestation tables. Skilled cabinetmakers, such as Hiram Pack at 488 Pearl Street in New York, came to the assistance of less talented mediums by constructing tables equipped with wires and other apparatus which enabled any medium not only to produce rappings, but also to move furniture about the room. James Russell Lowell was reported to have said that plain rapping was considered too mild for the spiritualism of 1853; at that time everyone was talking about washstands and bedsteads that were behaving as inspired. It was said that one man, a Judge Wells, was such a powerful medium that his furniture followed him about the room like a pack of affectionate dogs. [6]

Kane warned Margaret that she was chained to the dreary mysterious workings of the spirit world, and was permitting the professional coterie

[5] *Ibid.*, p. 49.
[6] Described in E. Douglas Branch, *The Sentimental Years: 1836–1860,* pp. 373–374.

of spiritualists collecting around her manifestations to make her a prisoner of their cult. Her talents, he said, placed her above the supposed-mediums who had espoused the art of furniture moving and spirit-handwriting.

In 1853 while Kane was away in New England he sent Margaret newspaper clippings commenting upon his lectures in the Boston Music Hall concerning his arctic explorations. These colorful, glowing accounts described Kane as a "small man, slightly made, full of energy, intelligence, and enthusiasm, and with an organization which makes one think of Damascus steel." Much was made of his choice language, modest manner, agreeable voice, and gentlemanly deportment. Kane's comment upon these clippings, which nevertheless he mailed to Margaret, was "How disgusting is this life, to be discussed by the papers! I need not be so proud, Maggie, for I am no better than the rappers."

Boston in February was cold and wet. Kane needed sunshine and warmth to recover his strength for another arctic venture. All his life he had suffered from a heart condition, but despite this handicap he had pursued a life of adventure. Kane wrote Margaret that although he was flattered by the fact that his lectures were most successful and drew around him all the "wealth and beauty" of Boston, he was nevertheless depressed by his ill health and because the crowds came not for the sake of scientific knowledge or for the sake of the advancement of mankind's appreciation of the great land mass to the north, but rather to hear sensational tales of adventure. He felt that the lure of Margaret's rappings was, perhaps, not much more degrading as a "sensation" than his arctic tales. He doubted that his audiences were really aware of the true substance of his lectures. In this mood, he sent Margaret a package of heavy laces by express. "Do be careful and dress well wherever you go," he wrote.

While Kane was in Boston Margaret, her sister Katherine and Mrs. Fox went to Washington, D.C. and held spiritualistic sessions in the parlor rooms of Mrs. Sullivan's famed boarding house. Kane admonished Margaret to remain the "gentle, quiet and modest" person she had always been and never to indulge in any spirit jokes with Washington people. He worried about Margaret's fate once she was at the mercy of the predatory male population of the capital city. "Never venture out in Washington," he warned, "except in the best company. If you get a real gentleman, grab him; but have nothing to do with the vulgar members of Congress."

Two weeks later Kane and his brother John came to Washington where they spent several days at the National Hotel; during this time the doctor and Margaret saw each other frequently. On one occasion Kane had arranged to take her to a dinner given by the French Minister Count de Sartiges, but she was unable to attend because she had agreed to hold a session for some friends of ex-governor N. P. Tallmadge. Kane was most annoyed at this. "Maggie," he wrote, "you are a d—d humbug!" [7]

Kane was jealous of the attention given to Margaret by such men as the well known American diplomat General Waddy Thompson of South Carolina, Senator Charles Sumner of Massachusetts, ex-governor N. P. Tallmadge of Wisconsin, and others who were then interested in spiritualism.

"Listen, Maggie," wrote Kane, "instead of a life of excitement you must settle down to one of quiet commonplace. . . . no more Waddys, no more Greeleys, no more wiseacre asses, and pop-eyed committees of investigation!" She must forego such excitement and attend school if she hoped eventually to live a respectable life and enjoy the security of a good marriage.[8]

Later in the spring after Margaret had returned to New York the explorer returned to Washington. "Your absence changes everything," he lamented, "the city looks like a forlorn village and the people like a crowd of ill-dressed pickpockets." Kane's irritation with Margaret for remaining a medium persisted. He was angry, as well, because congressmen appeared to be more interested in spiritualism than in appropriating funds to finance his expedition to rescue Sir John Franklin.

For old times' sake Kane visited Mrs. Sullivan's boarding house. He

---

[7] Fox, *Memoir*, p. 59; for background see Underhill, *Missing Link*, pp. 269–270.

[8] Fox, *Memoir*, pp. 81–85; for material related to Congressional Committees and spiritualism see *Congressional Globe*, Thirty-First Congress, 1st Session, XXI, Part I, 644, 684, 884–891.

found some stranger occupying the parlor rooms where he and Margaret had spent so many amusing hours; and the once familiar third-story room was now as naked and desolate as its white-washed walls. Even the garret looked sad and disconsolate. "I sat for awhile in the main parlor where the little priestess achieved her triumphs" over gullible members of Congress, he wrote to Margaret in a sarcastic vein; but the only old friends he saw at Mrs. Sullivan's were General Waddy Thompson and ex-governor Tallmadge. "Old Whispering Waddy" was still as lovable as he was silly with his mental questions; and the aging Tallmadge still haunted the parlor "with his sharp, cunning eye, but foolish, credulous brain." It was in this parlor, recalled Kane in his letter, that she had led these congressional buffoons around by the nose; and as the doctor sat there writing, he wondered if he, too, would be led around by Margaret if he married her. "Am I," he asked the young medium, "only a Waddy Thompson of another sort and are you only cheating me in a different way?" [9]

The next day Waddy and old Tallmadge came to the National Hotel to see Kane and to talk about Margaret. They expressed fear for Margaret and warned against the present dangers and temptations of her life. Kane tried to hold his temper at these intrusions and insisted that her excellent character and pure simplicity would protect her, but it pained him to have her life the subject of such a conversation and he continued to be nervous about the rappings. "I believe," he wrote, "the only thing I was ever afraid of was this confounded thing being found out."

Two weeks later Kane was back in New York as a guest of Henry Grinnell at the merchant's Bond Street house. While there he was prostrated by an attack of fever. When Margaret visited him in Mrs. Grinnell's drawing room one observer noted that the young medium seemed to be more fascinated by "a curious mechanical contrivance by which a little bird of gorgeous plumage was made to fly out, plume its feathers, trill a song and retire," than she was by Dr. Kane "lying on a couch wearing a robe of crimson stuff."

Early in May of 1853, despite Leah's objections, Dr. Kane obtained

[9] Fox, *Memoir*, pp. 91–101.

Mrs. Fox's consent to put Margaret in Mrs. Turner's School in Crook-ville, a small village outside Philadelphia. Mrs. John Leiper, one of Kane's aunts, and the New York merchant, Cornelius Grinnell, prom-ised to serve as Margaret's guardians while the doctor was away. She was sent to the little school several days before Kane was to sail for the North. The quiet of a country boarding school proved to be a sobering and thought-provoking environment for Margaret. She suddenly dis-covered a great fondness for the young explorer and was overcome by panic and long sessions of weeping; she suffered from an overwhelming depression arising from a persistent premonition that the explorer would perish in the arctic.

Receiving word of her distress, Kane procured from Mrs. Grinnell the remarkable mechanical bird and hurriedly carried this novelty out to Margaret at the school on a short visit which he managed despite his haste to prepare his vessel for the arctic. At the same time he engaged the illustrator, Mr. Fagnani, to etch a small portrait of the young me-dium which Kane later carried with him to the polar regions.

On May 30, 1853 Kane returned to New York and sailed aboard the little brig *Advance* on his second historic voyage to the arctic. Margaret was not at wharfside to watch the daring doctor sail away. A description of his actual departure, coming to her by letter from Cornelius Grinnell, told her that the sailing day was "beautiful," and that as the little "ves-sel passed along the wharves of the North River, she was saluted with cheers from the crowds assembled, and by guns from the shipping." The letter brought little pleasure to the lonely young medium.

At various stops along the journey northward and to passing ships in the near-polar seas Kane dropped off letters to Margaret.

Try to live that life which is its own reward, [he wrote] "startle the birds by talking to them instead of spirits, exercise at least three hours a day in the open air—wet or dry, rain or shine, don't be afraid to wear out your shoes, don't mope like a sickly cat, grow as fat as you please, and one thing more: should any trouble come to you—anything unforeseen, make ———— your adviser and friend. I need not speak his name. Call upon him as one having my confidence and therefore deserving yours.

When Mrs. Leiper, Kane's favorite aunt, came to Crookville to learn

how Margaret was progressing with her languages and music she saw
that Margaret's loneliness for her old life was driving her into a serious
state of melancholy. Dr. Edward Bayard, a brother of United States
Senator James Bayard, was called to visit Margaret. He recommended
a change of scenery and as a result Mrs. Ellen Walters, a sister of the
New York congressman, John Cochrane, invited Margaret to live at
her house in Clinton Place in New York City until she recovered from
her "mental disquiet." However, as winter came and hope of Kane's
return that year vanished the shadow of Margaret's depression length-
ened. Since she had severed her connections with spiritualism and with
her family, Margaret's only friends were those she had made through
her contacts with Mrs. Turner, Mrs. Walters, the Bayards, and other
friends of Doctor Kane. Her situation was made additionally difficult
because, with the exception of Mrs. Leiper, the members of Doctor
Kane's family were openly hostile and were determined to prevent her
marriage to the doctor when he returned from the arctic.[10]

When the spring of 1855 passed and still no word was received from
the explorer, official circles of the government became alarmed. A rescue
mission composed of two vessels, the bark *Release* and the propeller
Arctic, under the command of Lieutenant Hartstein of the United
States Navy and John K. Kane, a brother of the explorer, left New
York on the 31st of May, 1855, to venture into the Northern seas in an
effort to find a trace of the lost explorer.

While the rescue expedition moved northward the actual fate of the
doctor and his party rested upon Kane's skill in leading a retreat on
foot and by open boat over thirteen hundred miles of arctic seas and
miles upon miles of vast and frozen ice floes. The two years that the
party had spent in Northern regions had been endless days of hardship
and many disappointments. No news of the lost Franklin expedition
was discovered; and during the first winter their vessel, the *Advance,*
had become so frozen in the arctic ice mass that the ship had to be
abandoned. Thus, deprived of their brig, the party retreated to civilization by means of a small open boat which often had to be carried and

[10] The foregoing narrative based upon Fox, *Memoir,* pp. 91–116.

dragged over the many hundreds of miles of ice packs that separated the spaces of open water in the polar seas.

In September of 1855 Kane's party reached civilization and made contact with the rescue squadron. A few weeks later on October 11, 1855, Kane and his crew entered Sandy Hook to receive the resounding acclaim of the city of New York and of all America.[11] Margaret Fox anxiously awaited him at Ellen Walters' home on Clinton Place.

As the vessel came up the Bay of New York, Margaret heard the guns fired in greetings and wanted to go down to the quay side, but her excitement became so great that Mrs. Walters would not permit the girl to venture out. All that evening until midnight they waited for some word from Kane, but none came. When no message had arrived by midafternoon of the next day Margaret was in a state of great anxiety. She left Mrs. Walters' home and went to the establishment on Tenth Street where Mrs. Fox and Katherine maintained a spiritualism parlor. Margaret reached her mother's place exhausted and threw herself upon a couch.

Somewhat later that night Cornelius Grinnell called at Mrs. Walters' residence. Margaret was hastily summoned from the house on Tenth Street. Grinnell told Margaret that circumstances had prevented Kane's coming. There was "great trouble in his family" on account of his engagement to Margaret; he had been "beset on all sides by remonstrances of relatives and friends." In fact, the family insisted that Margaret return the doctor's letters.

The next morning Kane made a dramatic appearance at Mrs. Walters' house dressed in the splendor of his naval uniform. When he said that he wished to see Margaret he was told that he could not see her. She was upstairs—"the child was completely broken down." Kane kept insisting that he would talk with Margaret, but she refused to see him. Mrs. Walters succeeded finally in persuading her to go down to the parlor to see the doctor.

As Margaret came down the stairs Kane was "walking the room in a fearful state of excitement. When he saw her, he came near, clasped

[11] *Ibid.,* pp. 125–154; for similar details see Samuel M. Smucker, *The Life of Dr. Elisha Kent Kane,* p. 82.

her firmly in his arms and kissed her head and brow many times . . .
Both were in tears."

Kane finally told Margaret that all ideas of their marriage would
have to be indefinitely postponed on account of the violent opposition
of his family. He and Margaret were to see each other only as "sister
and brother." Kane then drafted a statement for her to copy in her own
hand which he said was to satisfy his mother; the essence of the note
was that the "relations between them were merely friendly and frater-
nal; that no matrimonial engagement had subsisted."

With considerable distress Margaret read the paper which he asked
her to sign; but after she had considered the contents for a few moments
she obediently agreed to copy the statement in her own hand and to
sign it, because by doing so she would restore the peace to his family
which had been disrupted by his attempt to intrude her into a group
where she was not welcome. As she did so, however, she reminded him
that "this is not right—it is not true."

Kane repeated that he had been worried beyond endurance on all
sides because of their intimate association. Now, it had reached the point
where he had to act for the sake of his mother.

Mrs. Walters then came into the room and bitter words were ex-
changed among the three. Kane abruptly left with the remark, "You
are not the Maggie I took you for."

A few days later Kane returned the note to Margaret with an apology
for having exacted it. Once it was in her hands she tore it in pieces on
the spot. Kane told her that his aunt, Mrs. Leiper, had seen some newspaper articles implying that he had been guilty of deceiving Margaret
and suggesting that the young medium had been caught in a game
which was much older than spirit rapping; Mrs. Leiper had then reprimanded Kane severely for his ungentlemanly behavior.[12]

In these unhappy circumstances Margaret resumed her old association
with spiritualist circles which by now had established a firmly organized
cult of believers and opportunists who rejoiced at the prospect of re-
covering their original fountainhead. In the view of these groups Kane's
interest in Margaret had been a pernicious plot directed by the vested

[12] Fox, *Memoir*, pp. 193–197; for related details see New York *Tribune*,
September 8, 1865 and Smucker, *Life of Kane*, pp. 193–197.

religious hierarchy to undermine the source of spiritualist power. The defection of Margaret Fox had been viewed as a blight on the new religion and her return to the role of a chosen vessel gave spiritualism new strength. The fact that the plot to cause Margaret's defection had been revealed for what it was gave spiritualism new momentum to move forward to the full fruition which had been ordained for the cause by the great forces of the universe. At this time Leah, holding sessions at an establishment of her own in New York as well as presiding over exclusive sessions in Newark, New Jersey, was having particular success with the wealthy but gullible of the great cities along the coast, and when she eventually married the wealthy banker Daniel Underhill, in 1857, she was able to turn both her full attention and her new wealth toward the organizing of "spiritualism into a new religion of enduring value."

During the following months Kane was busy appeasing his family, writing the two-volume narrative of his second expedition, and trying to keep Margaret from returning to table sitting.

"Do avoid the 'spirits'," he wrote, "I cannot bear to think of you as engaged in this course of wickedness and deception. . . . I can't bear the idea of your sitting in the dark, squeezing other people's hands. . . . The old year is dying; let its spirits be buried with its dead. Do write to me, for I'm sick and low spirited." [18]

Kane was indeed ill, perhaps more than he knew; in spite of this fact, he continued to call at Mrs. Fox's establishment to try to see Margaret, but he was denied entry. He appealed to friends of the medium to secure an audience for him, but with no success. The newspapers, which always carefully noticed the affairs among the spirits and the movements of the celebrated Dr. Kane, were most inquisitive concerning the true state of affairs between the medium and the explorer.

Horace Greeley, watching this unhappy situation and growing wrathful at the "barking and carping" of the press, published an editorial, under the heading "Doctor Kane and Miss Fox":

We wish the several journals which have originated reports, pro and con, respecting the persons above named, would consider whether they have

[18] Fox, *Memoir*, pp. 201–202.

or have not therein perverted their columns to the gratification of an impertinent curiosity. What right has the public to know anything about an "engagement" or non-engagement between these young people? If this were a monarchy, and one or both of them were of the blood royal, there would be an excuse for reports and speculation with regard to their relations to each other; but in the actual state of the case, such intimations as have appeared in the journals are not to be justified. Whether they have been, are, may be, are not, or will not be, "engaged,"—can be nobody's business but their own and that of their near relatives. Then why should the press trumpet their names in connection with each other? [14]

During the remainder of the month issues of the New York *Times* and the *Evening Post* carried occasional gossip items speculating as to the actual amorous situation existing between the two celebrated personalities.[15] While Margaret's friends waited for the explorer to issue a statement that would have put an end to these journalistic insinuations Kane's family in Philadelphia inserted an item in the *Pennsylvanian* which explained "the foolish story of the engagement of Dr. Kane, the Arctic navigator, to one of the spirit-rapping Fox girls." According to this version, "some time previous to the departure of Doctor Kane on his last expedition a subscription was started in New York by a number of liberal, kind-hearted gentlemen, for the purpose of educating one of the Fox sisters, a remarkably bright, intelligent girl and worthy of a better employment than spirit-rapping." It was in this situation that Dr. Kane had contributed to the girl's education "with a sailor's liberality." When the hero returned from his last venture he merely had called upon the girl to "witness the improvement of his protegee; and from this simple incident has arisen the engagement story."[16]

As the issue of the true state of affairs had now become a matter of press debate Kane feared that some angry friend of Margaret's would write to one of the newspapers revealing the actual situation. At the same time, despite his trying illness, he was at work writing the narrative of his second voyage while his publishers pressed him constantly for copy. Under this pressure, and because he had been promised a sub-

---

[14] New York *Tribune,* November 10, 1855.
[15] New York *Evening Post,* November 15, 1865.
[16] Philadelphia *Pennsylvanian,* November 19, 1855.

stantial advance which would make him financially independent of his family, Kane persisted, often working at his desk at three in the morning until "the letters danced up and down."

Late in April Mrs. Fox, having received funds from Leah, moved the establishment from Tenth Street to a larger house on East Twenty-Second Street. This change was made because Margaret had returned as an attraction at the tables. On the third floor of this house was a delightful little parlor that was furnished and set off for Margaret's special pleasure. On occasions Kane was allowed to visit her in the quiet of this attractive retreat. At other times, without Kane's knowledge, Margaret held private sittings for special persons in her little sitting room. One of Margaret's callers that season, her old friend the tragedienne Charlotte Cushman, gave her an ill-tempered poodle dog named Tommy who immediately took a violent dislike to Kane. Mrs. Fox and Leah also took an unkindly view of the use Kane made of the third floor parlor. When Mrs. Fox wrote the doctor telling him of her opinion with regard to the prevailing situation on the third floor, the arctic hero reacted to her letter with deep mortification and surprise; he would not for the world have "injured one for whom I have so high a regard" and would be the first to defend Margaret against "any aspersion which may be cast upon her." It may have been that Mrs. Fox was also displeased over the fact that Kane's monopolization of the little parlor and Margaret's time prevented the cozy third-story room from being used for more remunerative sittings.[17]

During the summer of 1856 Kane received invitations to visit London in order to receive awards from several British scientific societies. Since the publishers insisted that a journey to the European capitals could aid the sale of his forthcoming book, Kane arranged to make the trip, although he had prostrated himself in the effort to finish his book in time to meet the publishers' schedules. "The book, poor as it is," he wrote, "has been my coffin."[18]

On the night before he sailed Kane called all the members of the Fox family together in the sitting room of the house on East Twenty-Second Street and solemnly announced to all those present that "Maggie is my

[17] Fox, *Memoir*, pp. 270–291.
[18] William Elder, *Biography of Elisha Kent Kane*, pp. 231–236.

wife, and I am her husband." It was on the basis of this questionable "Quaker" ceremony that Margaret later assumed the name of Mrs. Kane. This half-way marriage was in some ways typical of Kane's earlier fear of taking the positive step of contracting a fully acceptable marriage in a regular ceremony. He seemed to be attempting to assume a proper obligation toward Margaret and at the same time refrain from offending his family.[19]

On the eve of his departure for London Kane was unaware of the fortune which his book was destined to accumulate. He did feel sure, however, that his literary earnings would be considerable. On the strength of this knowledge he made a will which allotted a large portion of his forthcoming estate to his brother John with the understanding that if he should die while abroad his brother was obligated to afford a substantial part of the royalties of his book to Margaret as her share of the estate.[20]

On the evening before he sailed Kane gave Margaret several envelopes lined with muslin which he addressed to himself in care of Boxman, Grinnell & Co. of Liverpool. Some of these he marked with stars which, if used, were to signify in a private code Margaret's wish for his immediate return; "whenever he received that envelope he would set out instantly, and would suffer no business to detain him." Kane seemed to be fearful that letters from Margaret addressed in her own handwriting would not reach him.

After making these arrangements Kane sailed for England aboard the steamer *Baltic*. On the voyage to Liverpool an ominous change in Kane's already precarious physical condition became manifest. His heart condition and the weakness that successive fevers had left in his lungs began to threaten his life. As soon as he landed Lady Jane Franklin rushed forward at the very shipside to care for the hero who had risked so much to rescue Sir John. Cornelius Grinnell, who was then in England, and other agents of his family's great trading firm, assisted Lady Jane in doing everything possible for the ailing Kane. When the unhappy explorer realized that his survival depended upon leaving the

[19] Fox, *Memoir*, pp. 270–271, 290.
[20] *Ibid.*, pp. 270–277; for corroborating sources see Smucker, *Life of Kane*, pp. 73–75 and New York *Times*, December 15, 1865.

damp, cold English Isles he engaged passage on the *Orinoco* on November 17, 1856, to sail for the sunny climate of Havana, Cuba, in the hope that nature's own warmth would drive the chill and malady from his body. Before leaving England Kane wrote Margaret saying, "I am quite sick, and have gone to Havana; only one week from New York. I have received no letters from you; but write at once to E. K. Kane, care of American Consul, Havana."

On the voyage to Cuba Kane's health continued to grow worse. By the time he landed there on December 25th his right leg and arm were completely paralyzed. He was put ashore and lodged in a suite of rooms in a small inn overlooking the tropical sea. His family was immediately notified of his precarious condition. And on January 12th his mother and two brothers arrived in Cuba.[21]

Margaret wrote to Elisha several times in care of the American consul in Havana, as he had requested her to do, but received no reply. The newspapers in New York carried daily bulletins on his health, but other than this public information Margaret had no word from the ill man. Cornelius Grinnell, who accompanied Kane to Cuba, arrived in New York some days later. In an attempt to learn more details Margaret asked Dr. Bayard to contact Grinnell who indicated that it was unlikely that the letters which Margaret had written to Kane via the American consul had ever reached the doctor, since his family, under the circumstances, was in complete control of the situation.

Margaret and her mother arranged to sail to Cuba, but just as the two women were about to embark the news of Kane's death, which occurred on the 16th of February, 1857, reached the port of New York. Under these tragic circumstances the mother and daughter returned to the establishment on East Twenty-Second Street, whereupon, from the impact of the terrible news, Margaret dropped on the floor insensible. " . . . No human thought could measure her sorrow. An illness of many months followed; and during the greater part of the time she was shut up in a dark room utterly inconsolable, and unable to bear the light of day." [22]

[21] Elder, *Life of Kane,* pp. 232–240.
[22] Fox, *Memoir,* pp. 277–280; for related material see Elder, *Life of Kane,* pp. 287–416.

The word of Kane's death aroused expressions of sorrow throughout all of the United States. By the year 1857 Kane was looked upon universally as an American hero of the very first rank. The remarkable success of the two-volume work on his second voyage added a brilliant literary lustre to his already heroic reputation. Kane was an unusual figure in American annals up to that time, for although he was the utmost of the gentlemen of the broadcloth pattern, a medical doctor, a scientist, a scholar, a brilliant literary artist, he was also, in spite of his frail body, a man of extraordinary physical bravery who had accomplished feats of endurance and daring in the far North that challenged the rugged, masculine exploits of America's great adventurers of the forest and Western plains. It was this unique quality about the little explorer-doctor which, in such a short time, thrust him into the realm of high esteem in which he was held by his countrymen. Thus, when his death became known to the nation, the American press echoed its grief as if with one great requiem.

The remarkable month-long funeral procession for Kane began in Havana. The Spanish Governor, the highest officials, dignitaries and hundreds of residents of the city marched behind Kane's flag-draped coffin. Accompanied by mournful music and ceremonial addresses Kane's coffin was finally placed aboard a ship bound for New Orleans.

On arrival at the great port city on the Gulf another gigantic procession carried Kane's body through the streets in a solemn parade marked by tolling bells and mournful bands. At every large city on the way northward the city fathers and other dignitaries vied with each other in a display of grief at the nation's loss of its polar hero.

A special train carrying Kane's funeral car moved on a route through Cincinnati, Columbus, Baltimore, and Philadelphia. As the cortege penetrated into the northern cities, drawn by a locomotive which maintained a steady tolling of its bell, the sad procession was greeted now and then with the booming of guns as if a great soldier were being honored.

At last on March 11th Kane's body reached Philadelphia to be honored by the most elaborate and climactic funeral parade of all. The greatest men in the state gathered to glorify themselves by showing a greater grief at the nation's loss than the speakers who had preceded them. After this prolonged exhibition of national mourning Kane was finally laid to rest in the family plot at Fern Rock.[23]

Almost as soon as the bells ceased tolling for Elisha, his publishers, Childs and Peterson of Philadelphia, negotiated an agreement with the Kane family to engage a professional writer, William Elder, to do an authorized biography of the explorer. Good promotional practice demanded that the work should appear as soon as possible. There was, indeed, another overriding reason for haste. The family wished to keep the name of the explorer from being linked any further with that of the medium Margaret Fox than had already, unfortunately, occurred. They feared that if an authorized biography did not appear at once some other book on the explorer including his connection with the seeress would surely be printed.

The author of the authorized biography, when it appeared in December of 1857, explained that the work was a definitive one; he had told the whole truth and had "not been obliged to suppress a letter or a line for the sake of his fame!" A New York reviewer, writing a commentary on Elder's life of Kane, took issue with the author's claim that he had told the whole story. It was clear, the commentator wrote, that part of the story of the explorer's life had been suppressed; the authorized biography "records only the exterior and gilded life of Dr. Kane." There was, wrote this reviewer, "a deep undercurrent in the navigator's life, which the distinguished biographer knew nothing of, and which the family did not place at his disposal." He was referring, he said, to "the love-life of Dr. Kane . . . A private correspondence with a young lady in New York." The reviewer complained that the biography would have been "more strictly true" if it had revealed the fact of Kane's "engagement there," which "he repudiated when he returned covered with the tinsel and show of glory because his friends thought it beneath him." In this, said the commentator, Kane's "courage failed him and he yielded his own higher feelings to the vain applause of the world." Here then, wrote the critic, was a phase of the hero's life that might have been mentioned in Elder's book. "And if the letters are ever published (an event not likely to occur, we learn)

[23] Elder, *Life of Kane,* p. 416.

another important leaf can be added to the biography which has just appeared." [24]

During the closing years of the decade of the 1850's, Margaret suffered from a continuing depression as well as from physical ill health. In search of consolation she often attended St. Anne's Catholic Church on Eighth Street and in August of 1858 she became a member of the Catholic faith at a baptism in St. Peter's Church on Barclay Street. As word of the fact that the medium Margaret Fox was to be baptized became known in the city a large assemblage attended the ceremony. To the correspondent of one of the New York newspapers on this occasion Margaret appeared to be "a very interesting and lovely young lady. She has large Madonna eyes, a sweet expressive mouth, a petite and delicately moulded form and a regal carriage of the head, with an aristocratic air quite uncommon."

Following Kane's death Margaret found it impossible for a time to practice the art of spiritualism. Her only income other than that provided by her mother came from the annual interest paid to her on a modest sum which the Kane family had been forced to admit the explorer had left to her. Occasionally, small items appeared in the newspapers concerning Margaret referring to her as Mrs. Kane. In some of these instances the Kane family sent telegraphic releases to the newspapers asserting that any inference that the famed explorer had ever been married to Margaret Fox was a pure "canard." Margaret endured these indignities because she was so ill that for the time being she wanted most of all to be forgotten and because she had been told that if she offered any contradiction the small interest stipends she was then receiving from the legacy left her by the explorer would be cut off. [25]

[24] New York *Tribune,* September 11, 1865; see also for similar observations the New York *Times,* December 15, 1865; Philadelphia *Public Ledger,* September 9, 1865; Elder, *Life of Kane,* pp. 3–4; Fox, *Memoir,* pp. 13–14 and Records of the Orphans' Court, 1865, Unreported Cases Files, No. 1072, ms.

[25] Fox, *Memoir,* pp. 13–14.

The Boston Apparitions

THE ILL-FATED Dr. Elisha Kent Kane had once written in a letter to Katherine Fox that "Boston is a funny place and 'the spirits' have friends here." This accord had been reached a short time after Heaven had sent its heralds to Hydesville, for at that time many citizens of Massachusetts had established a friendly welcome for the new ambassadors in Boston, Cambridge, and Northampton. The spirits first favored Boston by visiting small, select circles, but later, by 1853, large conventions of the believers were holding meetings at the Masonic Hall in Boston where remarkable proceedings were witnessed. Under the skillful guidance of the Reverends O. A. Loveland, J. M. Spear, and O. M. Martin the spirits of Benjamin Franklin, Thomas Jefferson, the Marquis de Lafayette, and Henry Clay, to name but a few, sent greetings and advice to favored Bostonians.[1]

Catherine Beecher, of the famed Boston Beechers, wrote Greeley that "after witnessing various tippings and moving of furniture and having

[1] New York *Times,* January 4, 8, 1853.

myself taken a ride around a room on a table with no apparent motive
power but the delicate fingers of a young lady resting on top of it,
I was induced to examine it further." [2] And a few years later, Harriet
Beecher Stowe, having lost her son Henry, turned to the spirits as a
means of contacting her dead child. Still later when Harriet went to
Europe, she communed with the spirits alongside her friends Robert
and Elizabeth Barrett Browning. Harriet often felt "Henry close beside
her" and asserted that her son's spirit sometimes struck a small Floren-
tine guitar that hung on her parlor wall; she noted particularly that
the bass string of the guitar sounded "loudly and distinctly." [3]

Another Boston brahmin who was profoundly impressed by Margaret Fox's liaison with the other world was the illustrious historian,
politician, and diplomat George Bancroft. During the early 1850's
death had taken his daughter Laura.

The loss affected him deeply [wrote one biographer] and he took seriously
for a time the wave of spiritism then sweeping New York City, searching
for some message from his daughter. He attended, with Rufus Griswold,
N. P. Willis, Bryant, and James Fenimore Cooper, a séance given by the
Fox sisters, the current rages, certifying their performance as genuine, and
he no doubt attended others as well.[4]

The Bay State, being a center of printing in America, produced
dozens of books and weekly journals devoted to the new faith. Spiritualism's advocates in Boston claimed that their faith had "rescued
hundreds of thousands from infidelity by intervention of rapping," and
healing mediums in Boston offered "remedies of ghostly origin" to
insure "health to the suffering at most reasonable rates." Nerve soothing
"vital fluids, psychomagnetic nostrums for bowel complaints," and
"harmonial-psychrometic modes of treatment" were available in Boston
for a world of sufferers.

The development of the new medical arts was but a minor advance

---

[2] New York *Times*, January 24, 1853.

[3] Forrest Wilson, *Crusader in Crinoline: The Life of Harriet Beecher Stowe,*
pp. 436, 450.

[4] Russel Blaine Nye, *George Bancroft: Brahmin Rebel,* p. 188; for two related
items see New York *Times,* January 4, 1853 and New York *Tribune,* January 24,
1853.

when compared to an event announced in Boston on June 23, 1854. A "Mrs. —— ——, the Mary of the New Dispensation" had on that day, while in confinement on High Rock, Massachusetts, "given birth to a Spiritual Motor" designed to revolutionize the physical world. The motor, issuing from a mysterious immaculate conception, "occurred after two hours of great travail." Only a few select persons were at first privileged to see the "New Motor," but later when the miracle was opened to wider inspection it appeared to be a strange engine made of zinc, copper, and acid which some knowledgeable persons claimed "heralded an event as great as the birth of Christ." A well known Boston doctor, J. H. Robinson, after examining the mechanism wrote long letters to the press solemnly declaring that this combination of zinc and acid was a fraud and that "the birth of a Motor," in any event, "was impossible from any point of view." Since no more was heard in Boston regarding the immaculate motor it is likely that Dr. Robinson's evaluation was a valid one.[5]

A few wealthy persons in Northampton, Massachusetts were of the opinion that a true *rapprochement* with the spirit world required select surroundings that would exclude the aura of skepticism prevalent in the Bay State. While not wishing openly to espouse the new cause, they were willing to provide the money necessary to enable Mrs. Susie Hutchinson, the Reverend T. L. Harris, and A. J. Davis to purchase a 9,000 acre plantation on the Kanakwa River, near Charleston, Virginia, to be used as a laboratory in an effort to "find a possible short cut on the road to eternal life." A colony of sixty Northampton spiritualists was recruited and sent southward to form the Charleston Independent Society of Spiritualists. This group of New England mortals, laboring for several years in behalf of a "whole-souled noble spiritualism," was not only preparing to save the souls of persons still on this earth, but was also preparing to go down into the lower regions of Hell to rescue the suffering misguided millions who had already fallen into those depths.[6]

While some New Englanders labored in the Southern provinces,

---

[5] New York *Tribune*, August 11, 1854.

[6] New York *Times*, June 7, 1853; for similar and additional material see William Hepworth Dixon, *New America*, II, 160–163.

other speculative Bostonians, noting the magic touch of the medium's fingers, developed the theory of "Digitality." In their view, the answer to the mystery of spiritualism was to be found in a full understanding of the "essence" residing in the tips of the fingers and the tips of the toes. "The fingers and toes," these philosophers reasoned, "are the seats of the spirit, the soul and the mind." The religion of spiritualism "is Digitality," said G. B. Giles of Boston in a long communication on the subject to Horace Greeley.[7]

By the spring of 1857 the spirits had penetrated the sacred confines of Boston's famed theological schools. A young divinity student of "remarkable purity and excellence of character had secretly embraced the role of a medium" and was astounding fellow students as well as the professors of the seminaries by his heresy. But because, wrote one observer, there were in Boston "clergymen, doctors, and sundry ladies and gentlemen who stood ready to testify to the verity of the claims made by the divinity student, the professors were forced to hesitate before branding him a fraud."

The remarkable aspect of the spirit scene in Boston, wrote this same observer, was

the impudence of those who claim to have established telegraphic communication with heaven, and the ease with which respectable and sensible people are induced to believe the claim. None of the feats that our modern necromancers profess to perform are more wonderful than those performed by professional magicians, who honestly call it legerdemain; and yet necromancers impudently call them tests and proof of intercourse with the dead, and find intelligent persons ready to admit it.

In such circumstances the seminary professors had to move carefully in curtailing the audacity of their heretical divinity students. To cover this break in the ramparts of the orthodoxy stepped the famed classical scholar, Professor Cornelius Conway Felton, and the equally famous Harvard engineering professor, Henry Lawrence Eustis. These two persistent and determined gentlemen attended every possible test séance held by the leading heretic among the students and finally

[7] New York *Tribune*, June 12, 1857.

trapped the young man into revealing the fact that he had been using "sleight of hand and sleight of foot tricks" as the basis of his "heavenly demonstrations." Armed with these facts, the authorities in charge of the divinity school expelled the "disgraced" student.[8]

Although the heresy had been thus curtailed in the divinity schools it was still raging in lay circles. To combat the evil in this area of Boston society, the professors organized a group of selected academicians designated as the Cambridge Committee to go out and meet the new diabolism in its den and give it battle. A leading medium in lay circles was a young nineteen-year-old law clerk named James Squire. The Boston *Courier* wrote that he was a "handsome, singularly well made young man," of "very prepossessing appearance" who could be compared favorably to the god Mercury. The feats which he performed on Court Street in the name of spiritualism were so marvellous that even the stern professors on the committee were shaken, and particularly so because of the young medium's "levity" and "high humor" when he dealt with the sacred spirits.

As the members of the committee sat in favored seats near the table, the medium addressed "jocular appeals to his favorite spirit to make haste with his work and not keep the good Cambridge professors waiting." Young Squire's favorite spirit was named George and on one occasion, as the famed classicist Professor Felton watched the proceeding with eagle-eyes and was growing impatient at the delay in performing some feat, the young medium exclaimed, "Now George, do it quick; I'll give you fourpence if you'll do it right off!"

This irreverence was "highly shocking to the learned Professor" who seemed "to hold spirits in great awe, and to be fearfully earnest in his investigations into manifestations." Horace Greeley's Boston correspondent, "Oliver," remarked that it was only natural that the young medium should be on free and easy terms with his spirit, George, who for several years, had night after night frolicked and gambolled with him like a playmate. The medium's levity in this instance, said the

[8] *Ibid.*, April 9, 1857; for additional related accounts see the New York *Tribune*, May 8, 1857, Boston *Courier*, May 23, 26, July 1, 1857, and for great detail see Hardinge, *Modern American Spiritualism*, pp. 173–194.

journalist, seemed to be a mark of "sincerity rather than an imposture, as the professors regard it." [9]

James Squire was not a professional medium working for admission fees; for many years he acted as a private medium in the home of "Mr. F——, a wealthy and highly respectable merchant in Boston who resides on Hancock Street, a few doors from the residence of Charles Sumner." The spirit George was said to be that of George F——, a son of the merchant who had been dead for several years. It seems that "George" had, with the aid of Squire, been revisiting his parents and also Senator Charles Sumner for about three years prior to the time when Professor Felton came on to the scene. The merchant, the father of the dead George, was at first utterly incredulous when the spirit of George first returned to his old home "and has only been satisfied of the reality of the manifestations of Mr. Squire's pretensions to mediumship by long and careful observation." [10]

Despite the setbacks encountered in the assault upon the baffling Mr. Squire and his spirit George, Professor Felton and his Cambridge Committee from Harvard continued to carry on "the warfare against spiritualism with great ardor." It was delightful, in these latter days, said one spectator, "to witness such chivalrous enthusiasm." Professor Felton deserved particular commendation, said this Bostonian, for "he devotes himself like a true knight errant to the extirpation of the foul monster, the dragon, the minotaur, endriage which is devouring so many of our young men and maidens—especially maidens, if those champions of purity, the Cambridge Committee, are to be credited." But whether spiritualism or orthodoxy would, in the end, prevail, remained a moot question; even one member of the Committee, Dr. Gardner, admitted that he was "not certain there were no spirits about." [11]

---

[9] Boston *Courier,* May 23, 1857; additional stories on James Squire can be found in the *Courier* on May 26 and July 1, 1857.

[10] Baltimore *Sun,* July 25, 1857; for still more material on James Squire, a very interesting medium, see the New York *Tribune,* July 16, 20, 22, August 4, 1857.

[11] New York *Tribune,* August 13, 1857; for a long detailed account see an item published by the Boston *Courier, Spiritualism Shown As It Is! Boston Courier*

One astute observer of the Boston scene in 1857 remarked that in his opinion the spiritualist controversy would last until "the present generation in Boston have individually solved the problem by becoming spirits themselves." At Harvard another ugly diabolism, professional jealousy, worked its way into the spirit issue. Professors who had not been asked to serve on the Cambridge Committee to combat the heresy of spiritualism took the liberty to judge demonstrations given by mediums independently of the Committee. It was whispered that, among these unofficial observers, there were several professors of the university who were "thrown into a very unscientific state of amazement at what they have seen and heard." Once more Horace Greeley sent his Boston correspondent Oliver to visit the wizards of the Bay State and make a report to the *Tribune*. This gentleman reported that he found the spirits and the professors rather dull and routine. He found the

mediums much more diverting than the spirits. The spirits are excessively monotonous in their style of conversation, [he wrote] and they are limited in the range of their ideas and actions. The mediums, on the contrary, are mostly persons of original and flexible character, cultivated by a droll, queer mode of life, and by much experience of mankind. A professional medium who has a good practice is usually brought into close contact each day with dozens of persons . . . they use their powers of observation notwithstanding the serious nature of their profession. I have met with no class more alive to the weaknesses and follies of mankind, or more disposed to laugh at the absurdities which occasionally manifest themselves in the best regulated circles.

Oliver told Greeley that familiarity with the spirits on the part of the mediums of Boston did not breed contempt. Several of the most eminent mediums confessed that they were "so horribly afraid of ghosts that they dare not sleep alone in the dark lest they should be startled out of their wits by some fearful apparition"; this was particularly true of the female mediums who generally appeared to be persons with weak nerves and active imaginations. One of the most popular male mediums in Boston asserted that "the spirits would not allow anyone

Report of the Proceedings of Professed Spiritual Agents and Mediums in the Presence of Professors Pierce, Agassiz . . . and Others, pp. 1–24.

but his wife to sleep with him" at night. On one occasion three gentlemen who "made the experiment of occupying a bed in the same room
with him found that they could not endure the rough usage to which
they were subjected by invisible hands." In one instance "the bed occupied by the medium and that occupied by his visitor were placed side
by side, a little distance apart. The visitor had hardly lain down before
the bedsteads were jolted toward each other and clapped forcibly
together, as you would shut with both hands a large folio volume."

Complying with Horace Greeley's instructions Oliver pursued his
research and fraternized with the leading lights of Bostonian spiritualism. Reflecting upon the professional burdens of the spiritualistic mediums Greeley's observer was happy that he had not been chosen by
"the Great Beyond" to be one of its channels of communication. Relax-
ing in the comforting nonentity of not being one of the chosen ones,
poor Oliver was, one afternoon in 1857, jolted by a sudden turn of
events.

It was with no little alarm, [he wrote] that I found myself the other day
apparently developing the table-tipping power with surprising force.

I had been [wrote Oliver] spending a long forenoon with a number of
mediums, listening to ghostly oracles, witnessing tables and chairs spasmodically jerking about, and feeling the velvety touch of invisible hands upon my
feet and knees. Wearied, exhausted, and hungry I repaired to Parker's for
dinner . . . I seated myself at one of the narrow side-tables and partook of
a plate of soup, meditating the while the marvels I had just witnessed. A
quarter of an hour elapsed. The waiter blandly removed the plate and
handed me the *carte*. I was perusing that distracting document when suddenly I saw the chair on the opposite side of the narrow table move—visibly,
palpably move. There could be no mistake about it. I watched it a moment
—it stirred again. I looked around; no one was within ten feet of it. The
waiter stood far off leaning against a pillar. The nearest person was a gentleman who, with his back turned to me, was peaceably eating his dinner.
Between us was an unoccupied table whose chairs were standing quietly and
firmly in their places.

I resumed my scrutiny of the chair. Again and again it moved, slightly
and spasmodically, as I had seen tables move when the spirits had seen fit to
exert themselves. I began to think that some spiritual friend, perceiving the
perplexity I was in about the *carte,* had volunteered to assist me with his

advice. In the course of my experience with mediums I had frequently seen advice given from the other world on much less important occasions. Taking up a fork I was about to point to the names of the various dishes on the *carte* and inquire, Is it that? Is it that? in the regular spiritualistic manner, when suddenly, beneath the table, a slight touch was laid upon my leg. It thrilled me, from its striking resemblance to the spiritual touches I had felt in the morning. Like them, it was soft, gentle, and quickly withdrawn. The affair was growing serious. Assuredly I was being "developed." In spite of myself, I was destined to be a medium. Already chairs moved in my presence and invisible hands touched me. To make sure of the facts, and to banish the last lingering remains of doubt, I raised the table cloth and looked beneath the table. I beheld a large yellow dog just rousing himself from a nap. His stretching accounted for the motion of the chair, and his nose I presume was the instrument of the mysterious touch upon my leg. I will confess to you that I made this discovery with a mingled feeling of satisfaction and disappointment, for though I had escaped becoming a medium I had lost a most excellent and convincing proof of Spiritualism.[12]

[12] New York *Tribune*, August 13, 1857.

More Gotham Spirits

GLORIFYING ITS victories and enduring its defeats, the cult of spiritualism unleashed by Margaret Fox meanwhile continued to grow in numbers throughout New York. On Sundays its devotees sometimes held spiritualistic picnics in Flushing, engaging steamboats to transport the hundreds of followers from Manhattan. At these frolicsome picnics "young men often wrestled with powerful invisible spirits" in violent acrobatic contortions, rolling upon the green, lush meadow-grass at Flushing. "Sometimes spirits took hold of younger persons and they danced furiously." Leading mediums and clergy of the new cult made speeches praising "the wonderful power of the human mind to reach beyond the barrier." Séances were held in which seventy or more persons united in a mass trance. Often the crippled and the afflicted came, and "violent effort was made to strengthen or straighten afflicted limbs even though no apparent cures were forthcoming." When evening came and the great throngs returned to the city some of the members gathered in private circles in New York, Brooklyn, and Newark. Critics called the picnics "fanaticism and sensuality" hiding behind the spirits and accused the spiritualist John M. Spears of organizing a Free Love order in which all members considered themselves spirit artists and frolicked in "the near nude." [1]

On a pleasant August Sunday in 1857, a large gathering of believers held a picnic on the grounds of Mr. Hoyt's estate at Winsfield, Long Island. A leading speaker at this picnic, the editor of a spiritualist publication, told the multitude spread out before him on the grass that he saw spirits daily at all hours. Occasionally celestial beings appeared to him "brighter than the sun," while at other times they "looked like dim shadows in a mirror."

When the editor concluded, a Mrs. C. N. French mounted the bandstand, raised her hands to the crowd requesting quiet, and delivered a discourse "with closed eyes and many grimaces." This "tall, spare, sniff-nosed lady after many jerks and contortions" told the audience that she had been "converted from the bosom of the Methodist Church" into the "warm arms of Spiritualism." Previously, "Methodism had had the power over her," but now the spirits guided her life. She exhorted all to pursue the spirit path to glory.

Unfortunately, before Mrs. French had finished, "a burly, dark-complexioned, shock-headed man rushed along, and jumped into the circle" of mediums seated before the grandstand; he "groveled at their feet, yelling diabolical gibberish, shaking his clenched hands, placing theirs upon his head and making mysterious circles around his head." The wise men sitting in the circle, after a sagelike moment of consultation, stated that the exhibitioner was "possessed by the spirit of an Indian." A very serious looking "clerical individual" who had come to the picnic as a skeptic told one of Mr. Greeley's journalists that this sight of an Indian's spirit entering another man's body was "miracle enough to convince him of the truth of spiritualism"; at that point, the

---

[1] New York *Tribune,* October 16, 1855. For additional material on the free-love cult see the New York *Tribune,* October 20, 22, 24, 1855; also see *Strong Diary,* II, 92, 93, 119, 125, 133.

journalist, not being of the same mind, retired from the circle area and sought out the lunch and beer counter.[2]

A year later, almost to the day, several hundreds of the faithful attended an annual picnic at Pleasant Valley, New Jersey. The steamer *Thomas C. Hulse* carried five hundred New Yorkers to the event, who, upon landing at the picnic grounds, made a "remarkable demonstration in the destruction of edibles"—a seeming paradox considering their "exalted spirituality."

Soon after lunch, a lady-medium, beautifully dressed in black robes and of "rather pleasing exterior, was violently seized by invisible spirits, and in an incredibly short space of time was put into a condition to receive an influx of inspiration from the spheres above and forthwith the group assembled about her" and received the word. Soon, rival mediums were "breaking into" speaking sessions in various parts of the grounds until the area seemed like a busy midway at a country fair. Many others who were not in a mood to listen to the spirits "adjourned to the dancing hall or amused themselves by walks in the country."

Later in the day, the Reverend John Benning an ex-minister of the Methodist Church addressed the gathering. He likened spirit communications to the recently completed Atlantic cable; there was, he said, at this very moment a great jubilee in the spirit-world similar to the renaissance which was now developing on earth. Soon these two great gatherings of mortals and spirits would meet as one in a gigantic reunion of the past and the present until all time would be as one and death would be no more.

When the Reverend Benning paused for breath the medium Julia Branch grasped the podium to caution the believers to keep away from side issues such as "free-love and abolitionism." These diversions, however interesting, paled, she said, when measured against the approach of "the spirits from the Great Beyond." Mr. William Robson, a visitor from England, arose to object to this evaluation; he quoted the philoso-

[2] New York *Tribune,* August 14, 1865; for another story on the same picnic see the New York *Times,* August 12, 1865.

pher Swedenborg to support the claim that nothing was more vital to mankind than a "liberal conjugal relation between the sexes."[3]

It was at about this time that Judge John Worth Edmonds made his sensational assertion regarding the sinking of E. K. Collins' famed liner the *Arctic* with the tragic loss of many passengers. This fine vessel was one of a fleet of three built by Collins to compete with England's great Cunard line. The sailings and arrivals of the three Collins vessels, the *Arctic*, the *Pacific*, and the *Baltic* were events of note in the city. Early in October of 1854 the *Arctic*, known to be loaded with many well known Americans returning from Europe—including several members of the owner's family—failed to arrive in New York on schedule. As the days passed it was clear that the vessel was dangerously overdue. The whole city spent the early days of October in anxiety waiting for a word from the missing *Arctic*. Eventually, the whole story of the tragic disaster reached the city, and it was learned that a majority of the passengers had perished.

Some days before the concern for the *Arctic* became manifest Judge Edmonds and his daughter Laura, by that time an accomplished medium, were visited in their home by the spirits of N. B. Blunt, Bishop Wainwright, and Isaac T. Hooper—all well known personages who were passengers on the *Arctic* then at sea. Edmonds saw them in a group. They asked the judge if in his opinion they were dead; he replied that as far as he knew at the time they were all still alive. Then N. B. Blunt told Edmonds the story of the disaster and praised Bishop Wainwright for his heroism and for the manner in which the churchman's fervent prayers had quieted the doomed voyagers.[4] When the news of the actual wreck of the *Arctic* reached New York City the implications of this spirit visitation related by Judge Edmonds in a letter to the *Times* caused some consternation even among nonbelievers in spiritualism.[5]

[3] New York *Tribune*, August 12, 1858; for a follow-up story on the same event see the same paper for August 14, 1857.

[4] *Strong Diary*, II, 133, 186–192, 197–198.

[5] New York *Times*, October 17, 1854 for the first account. For later follow-up stories see New York *Times*, November 13, 1854 and *Times* of London, October 28, 1854.

In April of 1856 Mrs. M. C. Porter, a spiritualist medium in New York, prophesied that the steamer *Ericsson* which had left the port some weeks before would be "burned to the water's edge before the 26th of the present month." This gloomy intelligence was duly reported in the *Times* on April 17th. When the doomed vessel failed to put into port according to schedule persons who had relatives and friends aboard the *Ericsson* had difficulty in suppressing a horrifying fear that perhaps there might be a jot of truth in Mrs. Porter's assertion. Happily the vessel arrived, her passengers and crew unaware of the doom which some feared had overtaken them.[6]

The brilliant Wall Street lawyer and famed diarist George Templeton Strong and his friends often attended sessions with the Fox sisters and other well known mediums.

I went off to 78 Twenty-sixth Street and had a private interview with Mrs. Fish and her knocking spirits [he wrote in his diary]. The knockers are much talked of now . . . The developments of this spiritual school have become very extraordinary and extensive. Beside their quarterly periodical printed at Bridgeport they have one or two newspapers in this city, and I believe others published elsewhere. There is a stout little duodecimo volume consisting of "communications" from George Washington, Jefferson, Andrew Jackson, Margaret Fuller, and a great many other people, all of them writing very remarkably alike.

The world of the spiritualists was bizarre indeed, wrote Strong, "tables loaded with heavy weights are made to dance vigorously"; it was "a strange chapter in the history of human credulity, at all events, and as such worth investigating."[7]

On a later occasion Strong was much impressed by a séance he witnessed at the residence of Philip Mesier Lydig.

Met William Schermerhorn and wife there, and moved tables. [wrote the diarist] Miss Maggie is a "medium." Her table answers questions by the alphabet. It was a brilliant performance, not obviously explicable on any theory. Very queer, indeed; no deliberate mystification, unquestionably.

[6] New York *Times,* April 17, 1856; also see the same paper April 18 and May 1, 1856 for related stories on Mrs. Porter and the *Ericsson.*
[7] *Strong Diary,* II, 93.

Could the effects have been produced by unconscious muscular effort of any person assisting? Hardly. I'm satisfied that if both subjects be not wholly humbug or the effect of an excitable imagination, both this and the Rochester ghost business depend on quite other than supernatural causes.[8]

And a few months later Strong was concerned about how the spirit mania, which had originated in his own state, had now taken a great hold in France and Germany. He hoped, he wrote, that European men of science would

investigate its alleged phenomena and either prove them humbug, or study out their connection with the facts of the visible world. If it be all delusion, the fact is perhaps even more important than the discovery of a new imponderable or motive agency would be. It throws new light on man's faculty of self-deception in relation to even subjects of sense. Rochester knocking needs inquiry in the same scientific spirit and for exactly the same reason.

A bit later Strong admitted that the sudden rise of spiritualism was "one of the most astounding facts of this age." The fact that "very many conscientious, educated, intelligent people" believed in the spiritualism made it all the more difficult for one to "adopt at once the imposture and delusion theory. It may be the explanation, probably it is, but if it is, the existence of the delusion is a most significant and important fact." [9]

After observing the same scene as that which had disturbed the lawyer-diarist Strong, Nathaniel Hawthorne wrote in *The Blithedale Romance,* "Alas, methinks we have fallen on an evil age!" If these phenomena have not "humbug at the bottom, so much the worse for us." Should these spirits be real, it indicated, said Hawthorne, "that the soul of man is descending to a lower point than it has ever reached while incarnate." If all this humbug be true, he continued, we are pursuing a downward course in the eternal march. "These goblins, if they exist at all," he wrote, "are but shadows of past mortality—mere refuse stuff, unworthy of the eternal world . . . The less we have to say about them the better, lest we share their fate." [10]

There were on Manhattan, however, brave men who preferred to

[8] *Ibid.,* II, 119.   [9] *Ibid.,* II, 133.
[10] Davenport, *Death-Blow,* p. 162.

meet their fate with open eyes—whatever they might see. A gathering of such stalwarts met in a "Grand Assemblage of Believers" in October, 1855 at the Broadway Tabernacle. The Reverend T. L. Harris, Judge J. W. Edmonds, the Honorable N. P. Tallmadge, the "high priests" of this gathering, pointed out that the spirits of Socrates, Plato, Martin Luther, and others "cried out to be heard" and many millions were now hearing them. Spiritualism, they said, had "made more progress, faster than any other religion ever started"; there were not less than "fifty thousand" converts in New York alone.[11] They come from all ranks, reported the New York *Times;* some who were very wealthy supported a large church at Number 659 Broadway where R. P. Ambler was the pastor. This "spirit saint," a "young man with sharp eyes and a full sandy colored beard" read volumes of Greek poetry to his congregation and claimed that "Christ was one of their own and so were all the great Greeks." The prevailing theme of his sermons was that since "the Day of Judgment is very near" the spirits of the great had returned to be near their former earthly abodes.

The editors of the great newspapers now began to fear that what they had once treated as an amusing humbug was actually not a laughing matter. After all, it was not a question of what was really true but what millions believed to be true that governed the affairs of men. They were particularly annoyed that men as respected as Tallmadge and Edmonds had embraced the faith and when outstanding Philadelphians such as Henry Seybert and Dr. Robert Hare, renowned professor of chemistry and trustee of Pennsylvania University, embraced the cult, many among the intellectual elite of New York began to take a second look into the phenomena. Dr. Hare precipitated this point of view when he delivered a lecture on November 23, 1855 before three thousand persons at the Broadway Tabernacle on the subject of "Celestial Machinery." He said that his discoveries in chemistry had been trivial when compared with his current investigation of the spirits. "There are vulgar spirits and good spirits," he said; "only the cheap and vulgar

---

[11] New York *Tribune,* October 16, 1855; also for a related story see the New York *Tribune* for October 20, 1855.

spirits" will work for "shoddy peddling mediums." His aim was to experiment only with the spirits of the "great." [12]

In Albany on August 23, 1856, reading a paper on spiritualism before the American Association for the Advancement of Science, Professor Hare said that along with Faraday, he had at first been skeptical of the claims of spiritualism; but independently of any medium, he had "set up a machine" of spirit communication and to his great surprise he was able to contact the ghost of his father who had been dead for several years. He reminded his colleagues that such men as Copernicus and Galileo had once been the objects of ridicule and he stressed the fact that persons living in the nineteenth century "which discredited the supernatural in all its phases" were "little prepared to receive these manifestations as originating from spirits." Persons who heard the famous Dr. Hare discuss this subject were left with a "feeling of shock and amazement." [13]

A similar feeling of consternation prevailed in scientific circles when John B. Fairbanks, inventor, patent attorney, and editor of the influential journal, the *Scientific American,* claimed that he was in contact with the spirit world. It seems that during the early 'fifties a beloved sister of the editor had died. As a result of this grief he had been tempted to contact the medium Margaret Fox and "from that time onward he was sure that at all times he was attended by good and evil spirits, and at length he believed that he was in sweet converse with his departed sister's spirit." Fairbanks tried to convert all his scientific associates to a belief in the validity of his new faith and "frequently communicated his opinions in the most exalted strains" to scientific gatherings, pointing out the ease with which those who were "bound to mortal life, with all its grossness, were able now to lift themselves above its material sphere, throw off the dress of humanity, and dwell in the heavens among the spirits pure and just, communing with the loved ones departed." When his friends tried to dissuade him

[12] New York *Times,* November 24, 1855.
[13] New York *Tribune,* August 26, 1856; for further stories on Professor Hare see also the New York *Tribune,* November 22, 24, 1855, the New York *Times,* March 20, 1857, and *Strong Diary,* II, 244–245.

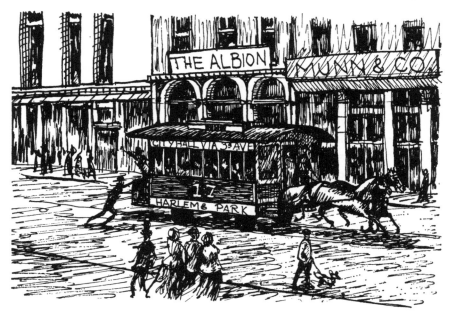

from making more experiments in this aspect of scientific phenomena Fairbanks "only shook his head in pity at their unbelief and smiled at what he styled their incredulity."

Early one Saturday morning, November 29, 1856, he went to a vacant room on the fifth floor of No. 658 Sixth Avenue where he lived. According to the coroner's reports Fairbanks sat upon the window sill of the room for several hours looking out upon Sixth Avenue meditating and reading aloud a series of "transcendental stanzas" which began:

> O' leap, my Soul, o'er
>   The gulf of time,
> To the dim and distant ages.

At that moment, a young lady living in the adjoining apartment who had been listening to the editor's declamations "heard Mr. Fairbanks raise the window. She immediately looked out and saw him falling to the sidewalk." The coroner remarked later that "it would seem that the deceased was so infatuated with spiritualism as to entertain the belief that he could at will leap across the gulf that divides time from eternity and join his sister in the spirit world." [14]

Disturbed by the fact that some scientific men were espousing spiritualism Templeton Strong wrote in his diary,

What would I have said six years ago to anybody who predicted that before the enlightened nineteenth century was ended hundreds of thousands of people in this country would believe themselves able to communicate daily with the ghosts of their grandfathers?—that ex-judges of the Supreme Court, senators, clergymen, professors of physical sciences, should be lecturing and writing books on the new treasures of all this, and that others among the steadiest and most conservative of my acquaintances should acknowledge that they look on the subject with distrust and dread, as a visible manifestation of diabolic agency. I am surprised that some of my friends regard the prevalence of this delusion with so much indifference. It is surely one of the most startling events that have occurred for centuries and one of the most significant. A new Revelation, hostile to that of the Church and the Bible, finding acceptance on the authority of knocking ghosts and oscillating tables, is a momentous fact of history as throwing light on the intellectual calibre and moral tone of the age in which multitudes adopt it.[15]

Professor Oliver Wendell Holmes claimed that spiritualism was a plague which had

fallen on the practitioners of theology . . . While some are crying against it as a delusion of the Devil, and some are laughing at it as an hysteric folly, and some are getting angry with it as a mere trick of interested or mischievous persons, Spiritualism is quietly undermining the traditional ideas of the future state which have been and are still accepted—not merely in those who believe in it, but in the general sentiment of the community to a larger extent than most good people seem to be aware of.[16]

In 1857, the New York Philosophical Society of Mechanics Institute was asked to undertake a study of the spirits. Although some of the

[14] New York *Tribune*, December 1, 1856; New York City "Coroner's Reports," December 5, 1856 (Number 1089), ms.

[15] *Strong Diary*, II, 244–245.

[16] New York *Tribune*, August 14, 1857; for a further evaluation of the force of the effect of spiritualism in America at that time see William Hepworth Dixon, *New America*, II, 149–174.

members of the society refused, a special committee of the organization composed of Clinton Roosevelt, George W. Glaze, John B. Whitman, John W. Reed, and James Chisholm agreed to make a private investigation and they secured the assistance of Mrs. Cora L. V. Hatch, a well known medium in New York who often lectured at the Institute. Her specialty was to go into a trance and then discuss authoritatively the state of affairs in the spirit world. "The spirit world," she explained on one occasion, "is a series of levels where folks reside according to their ability to believe." The great "harmonists" Mozart, Beethoven, Handel, and Haydn have a high spirit land of their own, while a drunkard "whose idea of pleasure is an orgy at Five Points" finds a similar place in the spirit world: his "spirit is a worm crawling upon the city's paving stones." She urged all "to live with a view to a future elevation." [17]

After considerable probing of the unknown with the aid of Mrs. Hatch, the committee produced an inconclusive report for the society. Clinton Roosevelt "added a Supplementary Report" which disagreed with the majority in equally inconclusive terms.

During the last years of the 'fifties just before the Civil War eclipsed for a time the public's interest in spirits, this remarkable lecturing medium, Mrs. Hatch, held large audiences at the Broadway Tabernacle entranced by a series of lectures explaining in detail the various "levels" of society prevailing in the spirit world with which she was in almost constant contact. "She is a slender girl," wrote one of Greeley's journalists, "who apparently has not been seventeen—the advertised age—for more than three or four years. A profusion of sunny ringlets and a fresh youthful complexion gives her an almost childish air. The peculiar position of her hands as they lay most of the time folded on her bosom with a certain shrinking nervous tremor in them, give an impression of sorrowful submission to the powers that be, which was heightened by the inexorable scowl of a powerful man who appears as Mr. Hatch, and who with the Reverend S. B. Brittan accompanies her to the platform." [18]

[17] New York *Tribune*, April 1, 1858.
[18] *Ibid.*, April 1, 1858; also see *Strong Diary*, II, 377 for interesting comment upon Mrs. Hatch.

A committee composed of Captain Isaiah Rynders (who later offici-
ated at the execution of the pirate Hicks), John McKeon, Charles
Westcott, and the renowned chemist Professor James Jay Mapes were
designated to ask Mrs. Hatch such questions as the following which
she answered during the period when she was in the throes of a
spirit-trance:

(1) What are the natural principles governing the gyroscope?
(2) What causes seeds of plants to germinate?
(3) Did the races of man all spring from one mundane parent?
(4) Was Jesus of Nazareth divine or human?

As these awesome questions were read to Cora Hatch in the hushed
presence of the more than three thousand New Yorkers crowded into
the Broadway Tabernacle, the gifted young medium was seated in a
modest chair at the rear of the stage. Once the proceedings of this dramatic meeting indicated that it was appropriate for her to make contact
with the message-mechanism leading into the levels of the spirit world
"Mrs. Hatch, who had been looking toward the dome of the Tabernacle, rose, and with fixed eyes advanced to the desk and made a very
pretty prayer . . . a rare specimen of rose-color pulpit eloquence."

Following the prayer the medium lectured for an hour in very general terms along Deistic and Swedenborgian lines using her shrill, but
exciting voice to "evoke remarkable drama" which left her hearers
bewildered as to whether she and her spirit telegraph had or had not
answered the profound questions put to her by the committee. She left
these wise gentlemen baffled by such paragraphs as the following:

From the great sea of the past we hear the murmuring waves come loud
and high against the sphere of the present, bearing on their crested peaks
the voices of ten thousand souls who have passed into that eternity which
has been all unknown save in the silent depths of the spirits, where awakening echoes find response to their singing billows and you hear the voice of
eternity saying to every heart "Come up hither!"

And following this celestial-centered essay she summoned the spirits
down to the Tabernacle in Manhattan to answer the questions posed
by the wise men of the committee. The colloquy which then followed
between Cora and the spirits regarding the four questions defied re-

porting. But the answers apparently satisfied the chairman of the committee, Captain Rynders. "The language is beautiful," he said, ". . . exceeds any preacher. I expected to be humbugged, and I'm agreeably disappointed. The theory of that is beautiful; I never heard the beat of it in the pulpit." [19]

By 1857 Cora Hatch was almost as famed a medium as Margaret Fox. The key to her talent lay in her ability to hold large audiences either in "rapturous delight" or to arouse vigorous opposition. Fervent Catholics and Protestants came to her lectures in order to jeer and hiss at the heresies she uttered. On one occasion a large audience broke up in a riot during one of her lectures at Stuyvesant Institute.

About a year later, in the spring of 1858, when a wave of general religious revivals suddenly blazed up into a second "great awakening," Cora Hatch was asked to deliver one of her medium-trance-orations devoted to inquiring of the spirits the true meaning of the remarkable revival of religious fervor then sweeping the city. On the evening of April 1, 1858 at Clinton Hall, in the glow of a hundred candles which cast their ephemeral light upon the entranced medium and the large audience waiting for the message, Cora replied that it was indicated by the spirits that the "great revival" was the direct result of the "economic hard times" then prevailing in the Northern states. Adversity, she pointed out, always arouses the latent religious nature of any people.

Every nation, however barbarous, has a religion of some kind, [she told her audience] when ignorance, of which are born bigotry and superstition, held the world in bondage, every stone, tree, stream, mountain or star was deified, and each was called a God; and ignorant people fearing their power for ill, knelt before them and prayed to them that they might be conciliated; hence, [argued the medium] fear is the origin of religion. In our day men are always religious when they are in danger. War, pestilence, and famine always induce religious revivals. Fear, [she said] is the basis of the whole scheme of the Romish Church; the priests have all the power, while the masses have ignorance and superstition; and the Protestant religion is the

[19] New York *Tribune,* April 11, 1857; for a similar story see the New York *Times,* April 11, 1857.

same in some degree, only the people are not bound by fear of the priests, but by dread of an avenging Deity.

Spirits, on the other hand, Cora Hatch consoled her audience, were friendly, tolerant, and willing to allow men in the mortal world to enjoy their petty pleasures.[20]

In the same vein, the Reverend Thomas Wentworth Higginson delivered a series of lectures on the new faith at Dodsworth Hall. He reminded his audience that spiritualism was but ten years old and the faith had come a long way in a decade despite the fact that Christianity had tried hard to smother the infant of spiritualism in its very cradle. Christianity, he said, thrived upon doom—while spiritualism's symbol was "the Summer Land." By way of illustration he described the depressing scene which one always encountered at a Christian funeral and contrasted this scene with the "happy and wonderful effect which was produced by the spirits at a funeral of a family of spiritualists." [21]

At this time persons interested in the possibility of fixing a contact with eternity and the spirits dwelling in that permanent but mysterious realm wrote to the famed German explorer—scientist Friedrich Alexander von Humboldt in Berlin asking his assistance in their effort to explore the great distances beyond. Humboldt refused to join such an enterprise. "I have," he replied, "a holy horror of pinewood spirits and parchographic mysticisms." [22]

Throughout the decade of the 1850's the cult spread across the land. Week long camp-meeting conventions were annual affairs in such places as Bucks County, Pennsylvania and at Harwick in Massachusetts.

[20] New York *Tribune,* April 1, 1858.
[21] New York *Tribune,* December 6, 1858.
[22] New York *Times,* May 6, 1856.

Spirits in the Provinces

WHILE THE CULT of spiritualism moved westward across the country, indicating that it was something more than a fad confined to cities of the Eastern sea coast, there were conservative persons who began to view Margaret Fox and other mediums as agents of the Devil. The elder Henry James had already declared that the doctrine was a form of diabolism.[1]

To support this view unsympathetic persons pointed to such victims as Matthew Langdon who cut his own throat after visiting a séance because he had become convinced by a medium that he would be much happier once he had passed on into the spirit world; or the Irish maid, Mary McCormick, who was poisoned by her mistress because that good lady had become convinced that the girl was harboring "an evil spirit" carried over with her from Ireland.[2] Two daughters of a man

[1] Henry James, "Modern Diabolism," *Atlantic Monthly*, XXXII (August, 1873), 219–224.
[2] New York *Times*, August 12, 1856; for a follow-up story see the same paper on August 14, 1856.

named James Ramsdell of Lawrence, Massachusetts voluntarily preceded Mary McCormick into the realm of the spirits in 1852, on the
wings of large doses of laudanum because a medium had pictured too
graphically the joy awaiting them in the land of the rappers.[3] Almira
Bezely, a rather amateur medium, received a spirit message that her
infant brother would die at a specified time, but when the doomed
baby boy failed to accept the fate the spirits had awarded him Almira
put arsenic in his bottle to avoid embarrassing her friends in the other
world.[4]

Critics also pointed to the case of F. A. Edwards of Equinank, Pennsylvania who, having received a direct order from the spirits to kill
his daughter and an apprentice-boy, tried to appease the supernatural
messengers by offering a sacrifice of burnt cats, and when this feline
fry failed to appease the spirits Edwards informed his family that,
under the circumstances, he would have to do away with the two
youngsters. Fortunately, his relatives, who were not unduly afraid of
offending the spirits, put "Mr. Edwards under restraint." [5]

Another similar incident occurred in Philadelphia in 1855 when one
morning John Crowley, the grown son of Mrs. Mary Crowley, entered
"the chamber of his mother, armed with a hatchet, and struck her
upon the head with the weapon while she was lying in bed." John, an
ardent spiritualist, told the police that he had been compelled by the
spirits to crack open his mother's head to let "some sense into it." By
chance, the hatchet was dull and left only two nonfatal holes in the
woman's head.[6]

William Love, another Philadelphian, had better success. Shortly
after attending a séance with Mrs. Farrister and Margaret Fox's mentor
Leah Fish in New York, Love had committed suicide because the
spirits had indicated their desire to have him among them.[7]

Of a less terminal nature was the situation which involved Mrs. Rebecca Schoenhofer of Chicago. Merely because she had tried to obey

[3] New York *Times,* January 12, 1852.
[4] Providence *Journal,* October 22, 1851.
[5] Philadelphia *Telegraph,* May 12, 1865.
[6] New York *Times,* December 12, 1855.
[7] *Ibid.,* March 9, 1853.

admonitions of the spirits, Rebecca was brought before a sanity court. A member of the legal profession who defended the maligned woman insisted that she ought to be tried before a jury of spiritualists. The judge ruled that while he had no jurisdiction over any inaudible messages that invisible spirits in his court might whisper in jurymen's ears during Mrs. Schoenhofer's trial, he was forced, nevertheless, to rule that her panel must be chosen in the regular way and not from the audience of believers in spiritualism who stood ready to offer their services. As the result of the judge's lack of sympathy the poor woman was committed to an institution.[8]

In the beautiful New Jersey village of Bordentown, a most remarkable "Spirit Marriage" took place on August 3, 1856. Since the bridegroom had died somewhat suddenly before the date selected for the ceremony, the young man's family and the bride-to-be, being spiritualists, arranged with a medium to marry the young lady to the corpse—or rather the spirit of the corpse—on the morning before the funeral was to take place.

The young lady, [wrote an observer] was attired in all the usual bridal paraphernalia, and after the wedding the funeral of the deceased took place. The dual affair was attended by over two thousand persons from Bordentown and vicinity, who were attracted to the spot by a morbid curiosity. The unfortunate young lady is the daughter of respectable parents who reside in Burlington, New Jersey.[9]

A few months later a singular figure from the realms of the spirits appeared in Philadelphia—a German-speaking "saint" who used the name of Anna Meister to conduct her earthly business. According to the announcement, as she entered the city on a mission directed particularly to women of German extraction, Anna Meister claimed to be the "Daughter of God and the sister of Christ." Her apostle in Philadelphia was Mrs. August Miller, "a most persuasive woman" who subsequently contacted a chosen group of German women "whose husbands were in good financial condition" and asked them to visit her house to hear the saint preach, an invitation seldom refused by the

[8] *Ibid.*, March 9, 1885.
[9] Philadelphia *Inquirer*, August 6, 1856.

ladies thus favored, as "it is not often that one is privileged to hear a sermon delivered by the sister of Christ." In a short time the saint had gathered together a following of over five hundred substantial matrons from the German section of the city who came regularly to hear "the Messages."

During the closing moments of each meeting the apostle, Mrs. Miller, would mention the fact that while the saint could not herself receive money, "in fact this evil would not stay in her hand even if placed there," it was, nevertheless, also a fact that money was needed for the "earthly comfort of the Saint and to insure her a safe return back to heaven at the proper time." Selected converts were told that if certain valuable jewels were given to the saint, or if a "particularly costly blue silk dress were given a cloud would descend from heaven" and "great revelations would unfold."

Given these encouragements, the good German ladies of Philadelphia gave the saint valuable offerings. Unfortunately, an unbelieving husband of one of the donors, discovering the loss of the family jewels, had the saint and her apostle brought into the city's Justice Court as impostors.

The saint, despite the trying circumstances of being thrown in jail and being forced to appear as a charged prisoner in court of law, maintained her composure insisting that she was of divine origin, and that she would "eventually triumph over her enemies and go to heaven in a silk frock riding upon a white horse, with Christ on one side of her and an angel on the other." The judge with little deliberation, sent her to prison to wait for the expected emissaries.[10]

Some orthodox churchmen, watching this growth of spiritualism during the early 'fifties and viewing the new cult as a threat to the supremacy of Christianity went forth into the provinces to slay the "Spirit Demon." One of these brave warriors was the Reverend C. Chauncey Burr. On February 3, 1851 in Bridgeport, Connecticut he faced the "Devil's advocate" S. B. Brittan before a large and excited gathering. Burr asserted, in his blunt and vigorous manner, that

---

[10] New York *Tribune*, February 21, 1857; this case was fully reported in the New York *Tribune* on the above date; however, additional material may be found in the files of *Anna Meister* v. *Pennsylvania*, ms.

all who could for a moment entertain the idea of spirits returning to this sphere for the purpose of rapping like so many frozen rat tails upon tables and chairs, were weak, insane, deluded, pitiable creatures, and fit subjects for a lunatic asylum; that the whole belief in these phenomena was attributable to the most willful delusion, and that the rappers were all a set of impostors and an ungodly humbug.

The whole of it, he concluded, was an evil marriage of witchcraft and jugglery. Since the audience was composed of a majority of persons who wanted to believe in spirits, this frontal attack ill-served the Reverend Mr. Burr's purpose.[11]

S. B. Brittan, himself a former Christian clergyman, arose before the audience and in a quiet, rational manner spoke to the assemblage as an advocate of spiritualism. All power, he said, "depends upon the mind; the spirit in the living was as invisible as the spirit in the dead. God's power was as invisible as the wind" and so was the power of the spirits. Tens of thousands of persons had witnessed rappings and believed in them. "If all these persons were insane and deluded," said Brittan, by that time having aroused his audience, he was sorry to say that many eminent Americans would "have to be included in Burr's catalogue of slander." There was much more to this epoch-making visit of the spirits than "the snapping of a great toe," he shouted. Tempers rose high and soon the "boiling meeting" broke up as the members of the throng left, vigorously supporting one side or the other.[12]

Shocked by the result of this bout with supporters of the spirits, the Reverend Mr. Burr undertook a long journey through the states defending the older churches against the "fanatics and fanaticism which was sweeping America." When he returned to New York months later he wrote a book on the subject which he hoped would stand as a warning against the onslaught of the spirit dragon. "For many years," wrote Burr in the opening chapter, "this country has been kept simmering and boiling with a feverish excitement, which I could see plain enough was adverse to all healthy progress,—Mormonism, Millerism, Davisism, and Rappism." He had embarked on his journey, he said,

[11] New York *Tribune*, July 24, 1851.
[12] New York *Herald*, July 24, 1851.

to slay this "legion of Ism-Mongers." But he had returned a saddened and defeated man.

I do by no means say [he wrote] that I found all the advocates of Rappism dishonest. On the contrary I want to say that I have found many of them strictly, awfully honest, and as shockingly deluded as were ever the modest victims of witchcraft in the days of George III. I have also seen many that were claimed as mediums who were undoubtedly honest—poor convulsed creatures half demented with excitement. Their whole bodies were violently convulsed, their hands and arms twitching and flying about as though they were possessed of the Devil, until at length they would begin to speak and declare that it was St. John or some other apostle, who was exercising them in this manner, as though he were trying to twist their arms and legs from their bodies. The whole phenomena is no more mysterious than hysteria.

Any intelligent physician could treat them, said Burr. But the sad fact was that dozens of these mentally ill persons were now being looked upon as links with the holy saints.[18]

In 1852 a medical doctor, B. W. Richmond of Ashtabula County, Ohio, was astonished by the sudden appearance of spiritualism in his community.

Our mediums [he wrote] are mostly young persons, and of a nervous, impressionable temperament. They are honest, and unconscious of any agency producing the phenomena; the mediums and the believers belong to some of the best families in the vicinity; collusion is out of the question; raps, clairvoyance and spirit seeing occur in numerous families. There are fifty mediums and more in our two towns and it has ceased to be a wonder; but it is not satisfactorily explained to the public mind.[14]

A few months later an editor of the Cleveland *Plaindealer* was also alarmed by the sudden interest in spirits at Bainbridge, Ohio. On Sabbath days, he wrote, "whole townships turned out, and the fields were full" of spirit worshipers and mediums. "These assemblages gathered without effort, with little or no notice. What does it mean?" the editor asked. He called upon the sages of Boston, the Buffalo doctors and such leaders as the Reverend Lyman Beecher to help Ohio

[18] *Ibid.*
[14] New York *Tribune,* April 9, 1852.

curb this plague. "Why is not this humbug, now five years old, but which numbers among its victims multitudes of believers in every part of the globe and some of the finest intellects of the age, exploded?"[15]

One Sunday evening in 1855, May 27th to be exact, a New York traveller with an interest in the credulity of human nature was taking a walk in the country near Dover in Athen County, Ohio.

I walked some three miles through a wood in the direction of what is called the spirit-rooms of Jonathan Koons. [wrote this traveller] I noticed at the foot of the hill several carriages by the roadside, and horses tied to the fences and trees; and on reaching the place, I observed from thirty to fifty men sitting on stones, logs and fences, around a dilapidated cabin. The men looked respectable and their deportment and conversation bore the impress of a religious meeting.

During his conversation with the men in this gathering, the traveller's attention was directed to a small cabin at one side which was called the Spirits' Room. He asked what spirits lived there and was told that "it was a room where people go to talk with the spirits of friends who have gone out of their earthly tabernacle."[16]

In such metropolitan centers of Ohio as Cleveland the art of spirit worship surpassed even that which was developing in Boston. According to the Cleveland *Herald*, the Ohio cult had eclipsed the Bay State worshipers by their "sensual and devilish" developments of the spirit doctrine. "A married woman spiritualist of this city," said the Cleveland *Herald*, "who embraced the advanced doctrine, has lately sat to an artist for her portrait, with no covering save her chemise. It is needless to say that she is of the Free Love order." "This person," a Mrs. Carrie Lewis, was the leader of a society of "advanced spiritualists" in Cleveland and had been given the "consecrated" title of the "Discoveress." The association had other important officers such as "The Financial Man," John M. Sterting, who acted as banker and benefactor for the society, and John Fenton, "The Builder Man" who was responsible for the construction of a great cathedral for the society which

---

[15] New York *Tribune*, August 11, 1854, quoting the Cleveland *Plaindealer;* for additional material see also Spiritualism Collection, Folio 21, Philadelphia Public Library, ms.

[16] New York *Tribune*, July 21, 1855.

was "a perfect copy of the human form minus the legs." This unique structure, which was erected in 1858, was designed so that "the eyes were skylights"; the building had "a front door and a back door; all the viscera of the body filled their parts in this edifice." Orthodox persons in Cleveland were "revolted" by the "terrible evil growing out of this fanaticism." The leaders of the cult, however, explained that their unusual ritual which centered around the worship of the nude human body was not fanaticism but the result of a discovery that spirits which would not ordinarily "hover around" persons fully clothed became positively friendly when a more familiar situation awaited them.[17]

Texans, not wishing to be slighted by visitors from another world, gave a hospitable welcome to mediums and travelling professors who came to Galveston and Houston on the boats from New Orleans. The Texas newspapers printed long letters to the editors concerning the verity or fraud of the spirit craze.[18]

A well known German in Galveston was seized by a force and remained in a trance for several days. At the same time "Professor O. S. Fowler, the greatest phrenologist now living" and the possessor of a superior knowledge of the spirits, had just stepped off the boat from New Orleans. After viewing the tranced German he declared that the man was seized by the spirits and predicted that when he came to the German would surely have an important message from the spirits for the citizens of Texas. A few days later, however, when the sick man regained his senses it was learned that the seizure was caused not by the intervention of heavenly spirits but by a "disturbance originating in the man's bowels."[19]

Texans interested in spiritualism tended to be violent partisans and held such strong views on the subject that the newspapers were forced to stop printing material on the spirits, because the violence arising from the discussion of these news stories caused gun fights which prema-

[17] Cleveland *Herald,* quoted in the New York *Tribune,* January 23, 1858.

[18] Houston *Telegraph,* January 30, 1857.

[19] Galveston *Civilian,* March 22, 1858; for other interesting stories of the role of the spiritualists in Galveston see the *Civilian* on April 13, 20, 1858, the Houston *Telegraph* May 11, 1857. Also see Arthur T. Lynn to Earl of Clarendon, "January Letter Book, 1857," in British Consulate Papers, as well as William Pitt Ballinger, Diary, October 5, 7, 8, 1865, ms.

turely transported a number of spirited Texans into "the Great Beyond."

On the night of August 31, 1857, when the nerves of some Texans of
Galveston Island were frayed by "spirit" and "comet" talk, a loud crash
was heard in the city coming from the direction of the Bay, which
frightened "most of the darkies" and "some citizens." A host of phan-
toms appeared to be about to descend upon the city from a dark cloud
then hanging very low and still over the Island. But tranquility was re-
stored in the city square as soon as the drays and livery wagons from
the wharves began to pull up to the entrance of the Tremont Hotel with
the news that "the steamer *Charles Morgan* had taken another crack at
the T-head of the wharf as she came in for a landing in the dark." [20]

Many "advanced" citizens living in the city of Providence, Rhode
Island, historically the center of tolerance in America, afforded an open
reception to the idea of a visitation from spirits. A prominent hostess
offering this welcome was one of America's leading poetesses, Sarah
Helen Powers Whitman, one-time fiancee of Edgar Allan Poe. The
poetess, having close social and professional connections with the "literary set" in Boston and New York City, became a leader among the "intelligent spirit-believers" in Providence. During the autumn of 1849,
shortly after the revelations at Hydesville had become generally known,
Sarah began to hear raps in her study and in her drawing room.

They generally occur in some remote part of the room when I am thinking of these manifestations. [she told her friend Horace Greeley] . . . Even
now, while I am writing to you, I hear a succession of slight sounds which
seem to proceed from the center of a table which stands at the distance of
four or five feet from the desk where I am seated. I am alone in the
room, and the noon day sun is shining brightly into the apartment.

One evening, on November 4, 1849, at a dinner party in Sarah's home
a séance was arranged with the thought that one of the guests might
unknowingly be a medium.

They all laughingly gathered around a large table in the center of the
room [wrote the poetess] when not less to my own astonishment than to
theirs we were greeted by a succession of slight raps, which presently be-

[20] Galveston *Civilian*, September 1, 1857.

came clear and sonorous, vibrating on the ear with startling distinctness in the midst of the breathless silence that now reigned throughout the company. The right hand and arm of one of the ladies became cold and rigid, and, by the advice of a physician who was present, we discontinued the sitting.

This incident produced near consternation in Providence among persons who were privileged to be told of it. One hypothesis of the cause of the raps was the presence of a lady guest who was for all practical purposes a stranger. This person had appeared to be the medium present and she had hurriedly "left town the next morning."

The whole city of Providence was then *hors de combat* over the matter of the spirits and "a large class of persons" were "compelled to admit that the facts" were "perplexing and mysterious," said Sarah Whitman. Some believed that the "whole thing was demoniac," others saw the raps as the result of some unknown forces of electricity. The "timid see Satan as the key," wrote Sarah Whitman. As for herself, the poetess said that the "demoniac theory" would seem rather the most "plausible," except for the fact that these beings from beyond were engaged in such "beneficent missions as that of hovering about us with messages of love, sustaining us with words of lofty cheer and inciting us to faith, patience and charity"—surely, this was not the work of Satan! When the Reverend C. Chauncey Burr came to Providence to expose this devil's business he found "quite a number of little boys and girls attempting to lend a hand in the movement of chairs and tables when the spirits obstinately refused to manifest themselves." [21]

[21] New York *Tribune*, March 26, 1851; for a follow-up story see the New York *Tribune*, January 17, 1852.

The Wakemanites

THE WORLD OF Margaret Fox was not without its fringe of fanatics. One of the most heroic was Justus W. Matthews of New Haven, Connecticut who willingly allowed himself to be slugged to death by a friend wielding a four-foot witch-hazel club in order to save the world from immediate and eternal destruction. Knowledge of this impending universal doom was transmitted to a select spiritualist sect presided over by the prophetess Mrs. Rhoda Wakeman. Her little flock, which had been chosen as the agency for directing eminently profound events, was known in New Haven in 1855 as the Wakemanites.

The death of the heroic Matthews occurred just in time to prevent the sudden annihilation of the world, which may or may not have been a matter of transcendent good at that time. In any case, New Haven police took a more ordinary view of Matthews' death. The Wakemanites involved in this remarkable incident were arrested and brought to trial. The testimony of the prophetess Rhoda Wakeman at these legal proceedings brought to light a record of unusual experiences.

As the prophetess came into the court room in New Haven on a December morning in 1855 she presented the spectators with a breathtaking sight. "She came closely veiled," wrote one observer, "and is the very personification of the wonderful woman that lived in Salem in the sixteenth century." The medium, a widow then seventy years old, had lived in the city for seventeen years and had borne seventeen children, nine of whom were living. According to her startling testimony she, at one time years ago, had been slain by her husband and during her strange death she was transported to Heaven for a personal interview with the Managers of the Universe.[1]

"After my husband killed me," the seeress told the court, "I was dead for seven hours and then raised; two angels stood beside me when I went to Heaven and touched me with their bright swords." The land beyond was a "place filled with red light and white clouds." According to Mrs. Wakeman, Jesus Christ came forward and talked briefly with her. And a few moments later she was put in charge of a "spirit" that told her to make peace with God, which Mrs. Wakeman hurried to do, not wishing to be at odds with her Great Host whom she saw some distance away "sitting on His throne in all His glory."

Then, when the angels took her back to earth she had been gone "something under seven hours." As she re-entered her house, she told the court, "I saw my dead body lying on the floor." By a manner which she was not able to explain Mrs. Wakeman "reentered her body." At this moment her husband, who had killed her, came into the room. When he saw her dead body rising he exclaimed "By God, she's raised!" [2]

The reincarnated Mrs. Wakeman lived on in her household in the usual manner except for the fact that she was in occasional contact with the spirits. In time, her husband passed on to whatever fate awaited him. After that the prophetess enjoyed a calm existence for a few additional years until her peace was interrupted by the appearance of one Amos Hunt who put an evil spirit into her friend Justus Matthews. This spirit, beyond Matthews' control although his body harbored the demon, had arrived from the lower nether region for the purpose of poisoning the

---

[1] New York *Times,* April 18, 1856.
[2] Rhoda Wakeman, "Deposition of Rhoda Wakeman," ms.

prophetess who had been designated while in Heaven to become the savior of the world. It was in these trying circumstances, Mrs. Wakeman explained to the packed courtroom in New Haven, that the heroic Justus Matthews had willingly endured the martyrdom of having his head bashed in with a witch-hazel club.

In solemn and stentorian tones the seventy-year-old medium reminded mortals in the courtroom of how narrowly their fate had hung by a thread late one night a few weeks before.

The details concerning Matthews' death were told in the confession of Mrs. Wakeman's brother Samuel Sly and the accessories Thankful Hersey, Israel Wooding, Josiah Jackson, and Mr. and Mrs. Almeron Sanford. When it became evident that an evil demon had taken up lodging in Matthews' body the members of the sect first attempted to drive out the evil spirit by giving the poor man copious amounts of tea brewed from the bark of witch-hazel trees. This noble effort was of no avail; the prophetess still felt the unmistakable pressure upon her soul being exerted by the demon living in Matthews' body.

Then, a delegation made up of Samuel Sly, Thankful Hersey, and Josiah Jackson went to Matthews and told him, "You know that you are killing the Messenger and that you ought to be killed." The unfortunate man admitted that his very being was a threat to the world and he graciously offered to do away with himself. Mrs. Almeron Sanford protested that this would avail nothing since if Matthews killed himself he would "be raised at some time" and thus the evil spirit in him would still be a threat to the world. Mrs. Sanford explained to the court that she "knew this to be a fact because the Messenger had had it by direct word from God." [3]

Samuel Sly and Thankful Hersey finally came to the conclusion that the only way to silence the evil spirit was to do Matthews in with a witch-hazel club.

In order to cooperate in this crisis Matthews came to Mrs. Wakeman's house and stayed in a back room on the second floor where the spirit in him could be kept under close surveillance. Samuel Sly went out into

[3] New York *Tribune*, December 28, 1855.

the woods and cut a stout witch-hazel club—which incidentally lay upon the prosecutor's table during the trial as exhibit "A."

The issue of what to do about the spirit demon came to a sharp crisis one night when the prophetess told her brother Samuel Sly and Josiah Jackson that "she would be dead in five minutes unless Matthews' spirit was put out" and that "if she dies the day of judgment would come at once."

Jackson went at once and told Matthews of this new and critical development. The poor man said that he wanted the evil spirit out of him. "You had better kill me," he said.

"No, Mr. Matthews," said Jackson, "we will not do that."

Samuel Sly then intervened. "We had better take the stick and knock this evil out of him," he said. Jackson was frightened and he left the room.

"I struck him with a witch-hazel club," Samuel told the court, "there is great power in witch-hazel. I struck several times after he was down; I did this for fear he would cast his evil spirit on my sister; I held up his head and cut his throat several times, and stabbed a fork into his breast several times. The influence I was under led me to do this; I was influenced by a wrong spirit to go further than I had anticipated, or had any idea of." [4]

When the trial was over the prophetess, Mrs. Wakeman, arose in the court and told the sheriff to tell the jury that if any of the Wakemanites were convicted for killing Matthews "the world would immediately be destroyed." The jury and the court, however, being fearless men, did their duty according to the law. Samuel Sly was held guilty and Thankful Hersey an accessory. The others were discharged with the judge's admonition to stay clear of evil spirits. The prophetess was taken away by the authorities to be lodged in jail until some decision could be made as to what ought to be done with her. "It remained to be seen," remarked the judge, "whether the world would come to an end because of keeping the Prophetess in jail."

While most persons were satisfied that Rhoda Wakeman ought to be

---

[4] *Wakeman* v. *Connecticut*, ms.; the same facts are to be found in New York *Tribune*, December 28, 1855, and New York *Times*, April 18, 1856.

kept in jail until the authorities could decide how to dispose of her case, there were others who rested uneasily in their beds knowing that the prophetess was suffering persecution. Letters sent to the editors of the metropolitan newspapers indicated that readers wanted to know more about Mrs. Wakeman's well publicized journey to heaven. To satisfy this demand Horace Greeley sent an editor out to New Haven to interview Mrs. Wakeman and secure full details.

Engaging a Mr. Lane, a son-in-law of the prophetess, as a guide the editor went at once to the now vacant Wakeman house to look for private papers of the cult that presumably were hidden there wrapped securely in witch-hazel bark. This search failed.

When the editor hurried back to the jail and told the prophetess that he had been unable to find the sacred documents she explained that the spirits had kept the papers from his reach because he had been accompanied by Mr. Lane who undoubtedly was possessed of the devil. She advised the journalist never to shake hands with Lane, for then the evil spirit would enter into him also. The awesome old Mrs. Wakeman then advanced toward the editor and seizing his hand, clasped it in her bony fingers; with a vacant stare in her eyes and a fiendish grin upon her old wrinkled face, she congratulated him upon his escape from the tormentor Lane. She said that she had it revealed to her from God that Lane was watching for an opportunity to murder the journalist and she advised him to procure a witch-hazel walking stick immediately as this weapon would prevent the spirits from murdering him.

The next morning Mrs. Wakeman summoned the editor back to her cell and handed him the sacred papers which she somehow now had in her possession. "You are not a man of sin, therefore I know that you will make good use of these papers," said the prophetess as she gave the package to him with the admonition that the documents must be returned promptly "or else the *whole world would be lost.*"

"Knowing how sacred she held these papers," wrote the editor, "I took them in a very careful manner and put them in my pocket, and bid her adieu."

The sacred documents revealed that for several years Mrs. Wakeman had been at times visited by saints and martyrs from the heavenly world

1. Margaret Fox. From Elisha K. Kane and Margaret Fox,
The Love-Life of Dr. Kane.

2. Katherine Fox. From Emma Hardinge, *Modern American Spiritualism*.

3. Elisha Kent Kane. From William Elder, *Biography of Elisha Kent Kane.*

4. The Fox House in Hydesville, New York (*ca.* 1900). Courtesy Rochester Public Library. Margaret Fox gets an answer to her signals. Drawing by S. Drigin. Bettmann Archive.

THE SISTERS FOX, THE ORIGINAL SPIRIT RAPPERS.

5. The Sisters Fox. From *Ballou's Pictorial Drawing Room Companion*, 1856.

6. Margaret and Katherine Fox and Leah Fish (*ca.* 1850). Lithograph by Currier & Ives. Bettmann Archive.

7. Turtle Bay, 1853. From S. Hollyer, *Old New York*. Courtesy New York
Public Library.

8. Cora Hatch. From Emma Hardinge, *Modern American Spiritualism*.

9. Judge J. W. Edmonds. From Emma Hardinge, *Modern American Spiritualism*.

10. Barnum's American Museum. From *New York Illustrated News*, 1853.

11. Headquarters of the Society for the Diffusion of Spiritual Knowledge.
Courtesy Museum of the City of New York.

12. The Spirits on May Day. (Above and on facing page.) From *Harpers' New Monthly Magazine*, Vol. VIII, No. 48.

Mr. Tupman finds himself at last in a very awkward situation.

The energies of our Vigilant Police being excited by this new mode of "Table Moving," the "Medium" is taken into custody.

13. N. P. Tallmadge and Robert Hare. From Emma Hardinge, *Modern American Spiritualism*.

14. The *Pacific*. From Christopher Lloyd, *Ships and Seamen*. Courtesy The British Museum

15. A Table Rapping Séance. Bettman Archive.

who arrived in her presence riding upon great beams of light. These exalted beings, after demonstrating how they had suffered in their time, explained to the prophetess that it was now her turn for travail. Thus it had happened that the prophetess had been called upon to endure much suffering and cruelty. In the course of seven years she "was brought many times to the point of being killed with knives and razors." [5]

In the view of her deceased husband, however, it had been his wife's diabolical nature which caused her seven years of travail, and he had often threatened to kill the prophetess in order to give the community some peace from her spirit deviltry declaring that the world would never be at peace as long as God let her live. And one night Mr. Wakeman had actually "killed" the prophetess. On this occasion he came into their bedroom and declared, "Last Saturday night I took my razor and went before the glass to kill myself. I made a steadfast league with the Devil that if I killed you he would clear me in his realms. I made the compact that I would kill you first—and by the great Jehovah Christ I will do it and they may execute me on the gallows."

And then, according to the sacred documents, Mr. Wakeman placed two chairs before a briskly burning fire in their bed-chamber; standing before his wife's bed he commanded, "Now prepare yourself to die —it is the last night you have to live."

"I got up and dressed myself as soon as I could," explained Mrs. Wakeman, "for I thought it was my last night. I spoke to my babe and commended it to the care of God, for I thought it was the last thing I should do for my babe."

Then she went to the chair and sat down by the fire. All the while her husband was cursing God and calling upon the devil in dreadful language. At the moment when Mrs. Wakeman expected to feel the knife at her throat her husband suddenly drew a burning brand from the fire and thrust it into his wife's body.

"It went into my flesh and bones," she related in the sacred documents, "and that was the last I knew of this world." It seemed as if a thousand little black spirits were carrying her away.

[5] New York *Times,* April 18, 1856; more or less the same story found in New York *Tribune,* December 28, 1855.

Soon a white spirit came forward and, after driving away the black spirits, carried her away on a long journey through the heavens until they came upon a brilliantly lighted area where "two angels stood—one with a bright sword drawn." Everything before them was like a great cloud in which Mrs. Wakeman envisioned all the evil dead who had passed on from the time of Abel's death—millions of suffering beings begging to be redeemed from the fate of a horrible death. But the prophetess did not linger with them; she rose in resurrection while an angel parted a great cloud and all Heaven stood revealed.

"And the first I saw there," wrote Mrs. Wakeman, "was Christ, just as he went to Heaven, with the thorns and wounds in his side, and the wounds in his hands and feet. Then I had great love and pity for my Lord that was nailed to the cross to redeem poor sinners from death and Hell"; and the Lord said "Go preach the gospel to every creature and raise the dead—heal the sick and cast out devils in my father's name."

After that, according to Mrs. Wakeman's story, two great angels riding a brilliant light took her spirit back to earth, into the bedroom of her house and returned it to her body which still lay beside the chair near the fire. "My body was cold and so were my eyes and hands," she wrote, but soon she was able to creep up, sit upon the bed, and eventually resume her earthly life.

After the journalist finished studying the sacred documents of the cult he returned to the New Haven jail to seek further clarification from the prophetess, before writing his report for the readers of the New York *Tribune*. The prophetess explained that her husband, during his lifetime, had been the prime man of sin on earth, but that when he died his evil spirit entered into all the world's people who did not believe in her doctrines. In recent months, however, the prime evil spirit had concentrated its power in the body of Justus Matthews making him the leading man of sin on earth. Her followers, therefore, had slain Matthews to annihilate the evil in him. Some members of her spirit group were still convinced, said the prophetess, that there remained at large a "number of evil spirits in different men of sin." Some day her followers would seek out and put to death these harborers of evil being; but for the time being Mrs. Wakeman advised the readers of Greeley's *Tribune* to brew themselves an occasional cup of tea made from the bark of a witch-hazel tree in order to keep their bodies free of evil spirits. And as a result of this advice which was given some notice in the press several enterprising merchants in New York added this item to their stocks.[6]

But the governmental authorities in Connecticut, having little fear of evil spirits, kept the prophetess confined in a state institution for the insane, and the cult of the Wakemanites soon withered on the vine. In 1859 the prophetess passed on once again into the white clouds of the hereafter—free, one may hope, from evil spirits and sin.[7]

[6] New York *Tribune,* December 28, 1855.

[7] New York *Times,* April 18, 1856. For some additional details on the Wakemanites see New Haven *Journal and Courier,* December 27, 1855.

The Ghost in the Astor Library

As the fantasy of Margaret Fox continued to invade the minds of people in America, spiritualism became the concern of some scholars in high places.

The Astor Library, first established on Lafayette Square and a forerunner of the great institution at 42nd Street and Fifth Avenue in New York City, was one of the many monuments left to the city by William B. Astor. In the year 1860 the Astor Library was the site of a remarkable spiritualistic manifestation which came to be known in private circles in New York City as "Doctor Cogswell's Spirit-ghost at the Astor." Dr. Cogswell, a famed scholar, was the confidant of such illustrious historians as George Bancroft and William H. Prescott, friend of George Templeton Strong and Ralph Waldo Emerson, beneficiary of the Astor family, and the eminent librarian whose bibliographical genius still adorns the catalogue of the great library which now stands at Fifth Avenue and 42nd Street.

Dr. Joseph Green Cogswell was a hardheaded, monklike bachelor who devoted his life to building the Astor collection. One of the prized holdings of the library at that time pertained to spiritualism and necromancy. The learned tomes upon this subject which Dr. Cogswell had collected reach almost as far back as the history of the written word.

During the daylight hours of those decades long ago Cogswell busied himself with the usual tasks of the librarian, but after sundown he lighted his candle and engaged his great energy in the enormous task of cataloging the Astor Collection.

Although for several weeks during the early winter days of 1860 there had been "a bit of gossip uptown" concerning demonology and witchcraft at the Astor Library, it seemed incredible that these "comfortable, well lighted spacious halls" could house "spirit demons"; it was preposterous to assume that the spacious corridors, which in daylight were "enlivened by gaily dressed lady visitors" with their musically laughing voices, could be haunted by a spectre at night. Yet a scholarly gentleman who was cognizant of Dr. Cogswell's real dilemma at the Astor once asked skeptics to

imagine these wide halls as they are at night swathed in darkness, the gloomy alcoves casting yet deeper and gloomier shadows—when a footfall reverberates through the wide expanse with mysterious echoes, and when the lamps borne by the startled explorer along the tortuous passages and among the musty tomes sends but a feeble ray that scarcely serves to make the darkness visible; at such a time the aspect is very different.

It was in such gloomy circumstances, said this narrator, that the librarian first began to be harassed by supernatural demons. Dr. Cogswell, being an unmarried man, occupied a sleeping apartment in the upper part of the library. Against the advice of his friends he devoted many of his night hours to his work on the catalogue; he was so anxious to hasten the completion of the work and fired with all the enthusiasm of a professed bibliophile, that his labors in this tedious work were almost incredible. His friends acknowledged that the "dry statistical character of the bibliographer's work" was by no means "suggestive of fanciful apparitions," nor could an experienced compiler, such as Dr. Cogswell, be easily swayed by "passing delusions of the eye or brain."

In the face of all these considerations, Dr. Cogswell's encounter with

a spectre became still more inexplicable. The whole story of his encounter with the agents of the supernatural was related by him one evening
on the last day of February of the year 1860. The occasion appears to
have been a dinner party at the home of William B. Astor in New York
City. The guests in this instance included the host plus John Astor,
George Templeton Strong, Horace Greeley, George Bancroft, Tom
Ludlow, George Ticknor, Dr. Cogswell, and many other literary personages in the city.[1]

It seems that one evening, at about eleven o'clock at night while Dr.
Cogswell was at work in the stacks writing his library cards, he had an
occasion to refer to some books in a distant part of the building. According to the narrative, as related by one of the dinner guests, the doctor took his candle, as he had often done before, and pursued his course
among the winding passages toward the desired shelf. Before reaching
it, while in an alcove in the southwest part of the older portion of the
building, he was startled by seeing a man, respectably dressed in citizen's clothes, surveying a shelf of books. The doctor supposed it to be a
robber who had secreted himself for the purpose of abstracting some of
the valuable works of the library. After stepping behind a partition for
a moment, the librarian again moved cautiously forward to catch a
glimpse of the individual's face; to his surprise he recognized in the
supposed robber the features of a well known physician who once lived
in the vicinity of the library, and who had died some six weeks earlier!
It should be borne in mind that the deceased person was a mere acquaintance of Dr. Cogswell, not an intimate friend, and since his death
Dr. Cogswell had not thought of him.

The librarian not being a man easily frightened calmly addressed the
spirit. "Doctor," he said, "you seldom if ever visited this library while
living. Why do you now trouble us while dead?" Perhaps the ghost
did not like the sound of the human voice; in any case, it gave no answer, but disappeared.

The next day, according to the story as told by the librarian's friend,
Dr. Cogswell thought the matter over and attributed it to some optical
delusion, and in the evening proceeded with his work as usual. Again

---

[1] Most of this tale of the experience of Dr. Cogswell is found in a long story
in the New York *Tribune* of March 13, 1860.

he wished to refer to some books, and visited the western alcove. There again, as large as life was the spirit, very calmly, and placidly surveying the shelves.

"Doctor," inquired the librarian, "again I ask you, why you, who never visited the library while living, trouble it now when dead?"

Once more the ghost vanished. The next day Dr. Cogswell examined the shelves before which the apparition had been standing, found that, by a singular coincidence, the shelves which had interested the spirit were filled with books devoted to demonology, witchcraft, magic, and spiritualism. Some of these books were "rare tomes, several centuries old, written in Latin, illustrated with quaint diagrams, and redolent of mysticism; while on the next shelves were the younger brethren, the neat spruce works of modern spiritualists, of Brittan, Davis, Edmonds, and others." [2]

The very titles of these mystic books were suggestive, Dr. Cogswell told the astonished guests at Astor's dinner party that night in 1860. On the shelves which interested the spirit of the former physician, he said,

are the prophecies or prognostications of Michael Nostradamus, a folio published in London in 1672; Albamazar's *de Conjectionibus;* Kerner's *Mayiken;* Godwin's *Lives of the Necromancers;* Glanvil on witches and apparitions; Cornelius Agrippa; Bodkin's *Demonomania;* Lilly's *Astrology,* and others, a perusal of which would effectually murder the sleep of a person of ordinary nerve for at least a dozen nights. It was these volumes that appeared to attract the apparition. [3]

Despite his strange experiences the librarian determined to continue his labors of constructing a catalogue. The occasion once more arose when he had to pass the haunted alcove, and he again encountered the apparition "dressed as before, in a gentleman's costume, as natural as life, and with a hand raised as if to take down a book."

Again Cogswell spoke. "Doctor," he said boldly, "this is the third time I have met you. Tell me if any class of books here now disturb you? If they do I will have them removed."

[2] *Ibid.;* also see "Joseph Green Cogswell," Allen Johnson and Dumas Malone (eds.), *Dictionary of American Biography,* IV, 273–274.

[3] *Ibid.* A more general story of the same incident of the ghost can be found in the New York *Evening Post* of March 10, 11, 12, 1860.

The ungrateful spirit, even without acknowledging the cooperative approach of the librarian, disappeared into the darkness behind the light of Cogswell's flickering candle; nor did he ever reappear again although the librarian afterwards often approached the same alcove.

When Doctor Cogswell finished telling of this remarkable experience to the many assembled guests at the dinner party, some of the illustrious persons present attributed "Cogswell's ghost seeing to the strain and tension of his nerves during his too protracted labors at the catalogue"; still others admitted that the story had "its remarkable phases." All agreed that both "Cogswell and the deceased physician were persons of a practical turn of mind" who had "always treated the marvellous spirit stories sometimes set afloat with contempt; and as the two were never at all intimate" it was at least a curious question "for the psychologist to determine why the idea of this deceased gentleman should come to Mr. Cogswell's brain and resolve itself into an apparition, when engaged in statistical labors, which should effectively banish all thoughts of the marvellous."

Not being able to give the good librarian, Doctor Cogswell, a rational explanation of the shattering experience which he had endured, his friends sent him away on a short trip to Charleston, South Carolina where it was hoped the mild sea air would enable him to forget the apparition and recover his "indefatigable industry, his devotion to the interests of the Astor Library, and his great efficiency as a librarian." The fact that Cogswell's great catalogue later progressed from the letter "P" upon which he had been working when interrupted by the spectre to the finality of the letter "Z" would seem to indicate that the good bibliographer, with the aid of the balmy Southern sea breezes, eventually recovered his equilibrium and recommenced his truly titanic labor.[4]

[4] New York *Tribune*, March 13, 1860; also see *Strong Diary*, II, 273, 336.

Congress and Spiritualism

As THE BELIEVERS in spiritualism increased in numbers—totaling in the mid-1850's about ten million—the politicians began to consider "the spiritualist vote." The hundreds of mediums and circles in the provinces were avid letter writers, petition signers, and composers of memorials and all of these polemic devices were used to induce the lawmakers to consider the issues arising from the hovering spirits. The parlor rooms of the famed boarding-houses, gaming rooms, and other establishments of merriment in Washington had their table-sitting mediums and rappers. Here congressmen who gathered for sport were often seriously moved by the "astonishing peculiarities" that occurred in the "eerie, frolicksome darkness" as the solons sat around a table presided over by a "fair female medium"—who sometimes happened to be Margaret Fox.[1]

While most of the lawmakers publicly professed to be only amused by the strange phenomena it was likely that many of these scoffers were

[1] Fox, *Memoir*, pp. 80–97.

at times gravely uncertain as to whether or not they should take a more serious note of the spirits. In any case, Washington patronized the mediums more generously than other large American cities.[2] The famed correspondent of the *Times* of London, William H. Russell, on a visit to Washington noted that it was

strange to see in journals which profess to represent civilization and intelligence of the most enlightened and highly educated people on the face of the earth, advertisements of sorcerers, wizards, fortune-tellers by the score, "wonderful clairvoyants," the "seventh child of a seventh child," "mesmeristic necromancers" and the like who can tell your thoughts as soon as you enter the room, and secure the affections you prize, give lucky numbers, and make everybody's fortune but their own.[3]

The mediums in Washington served the lawmakers in many ways. Dr. B. W. Richmond wrote that a friend of his, a United States senator from Ohio, received an important letter much of which was written in an illegible hand. The senator consulted his medium who told him to bind the letter to his forehead; once this had been done the content of the letter was revealed to the lawmaker with the aid of friendly spirits called up by the medium. Extending this process, the delighted senator endeavored to get long Senate documents worked into his head in this painless manner but with little noticeable success.[4]

Early in February of 1853, before the death of Dr. Kane, Mrs. Fox had taken Margaret away from the manifestation establishment on Twenty-Sixth Street in New York and moved their operations to Washington for a short professional visit in the capital city. The former governor of Wisconsin, N. P. Tallmadge, an ardent spiritualist, secured lodgings for the Foxes at Mrs. Sullivan's at F. Street and 13th, a well known boarding-house in the city which was patronized by army officers and members of Congress, many of whom came to the sittings under an influence of spirits which arose not from the art of the table rappers, but from that of the brewers.[5]

[2] Carl Sandburg, *Abraham Lincoln: The War Years*, III, 345. New York *Tribune*, November 16, 1858.
[3] New York *Tribune*, November 5, 1858.
[4] New York *Tribune*, May 22, 1852.
[5] Fox, *Memoir*, pp. 59–69.

Katherine wrote Leah at this time saying that "last evening a party of fine-looking gentlemen visited our rooms. All, but two, were as drunk as they could well be. They made mean, low remarks." Margaret immediately left the room. "Imagine," wrote Katherine, "Maggie and me, and dear Mother, before a crowd of drunken senators!" One very fine-looking senator stood up and addressed the gathering. "I wish to be heard, gentlemen. This is all a humbug, but it's worth a dollar" to look into the eyes of the young Fox ladies. One young naval officer wanted Margaret to return; he was most persistent. Finally, one of his friends told Katherine and Mrs. Fox not to be offended. "Don't mind him," the friend said, "he is drunk; I would not pay the least attention to him. He is a gentleman and when I repeat his language to him tomorrow he will feel ashamed of his conduct." It was a horrid scene, wrote Katherine, which ended only after the Fox girls had left the room.[6]

Several prominent public men in Washington who were firm believers in spiritualism were energetic, proselytizing lobbyists for the faith in the halls of Congress. Ex-governor Tallmadge was one of these; so was his friend General Waddy Thompson, the illustrious diplomat, former ambassador to Mexico, and a member of one of Carolina's foremost families. Judge John Worth Edmonds of New York also spent much time in Washington for the cause. And in the Congress itself Senator James Shields of Illinois and Charles Sumner of Massachusetts, under pressure from the spiritualist vote presented petitions and memorials in the interest of spiritualism.[7]

On April 17, 1854, Senator Shields presented a petition signed by fifteen thousand of his spiritualist constituents who wanted the Congress to finance an official commission to make a study of the apparent attempt by beings of the other world to set up an actual liaison with the mortal world. After reading a summary of the petition the senator spoke to his colleagues supporting the plea:

SPIRITUAL MANIFESTATIONS

Mr. Shields. Mr. President, I beg leave to present to the Senate a petition, with some fifteen thousand names appended to it, upon a very singular and

---

[6] *Ibid.*   [7] New York *Tribune,* March 28, 1859.

novel subject. The petitioners represent, that certain physical and mental phenomena of mysterious import have become so prevalent in this country and Europe as to engross a large share of public attention.

A partial analysis of these phenomena attest the existence:

First. Of an "occult force," which is exhibited in sliding, raising, arresting, holding, suspending, and otherwise disturbing ponderable bodies, apparently in direct opposition to the acknowledged laws of matter; and transcending the accredited powers of the human mind.

Secondly. Lights of various forms and colors, and of different degrees of intensity, appear in dark rooms, where chemical action, or phosphorescent illumination, cannot be developed, and where there are no means of generating electricity, or of producing combustion.

Thirdly. A variety of sounds, frequent in occurrence, and diversified in character, and of singular significance and import, consisting of mysterious rappings, indicating the presence of invisible intelligence. Sounds are often heard like those produced by the prosecution of mechanical operations—like the hoarse murmurs of the winds and waves, mingled with the harsh creaking noise of the masts and rigging of a ship laboring in a rough sea. Concussions also occur, resembling distant thunder, producing oscillatory movements of surrounding objects, and a tremulous motion of the premises upon which these phenomena occur. Harmonious sounds as of human voices, and other sounds resembling those of the fife, drum, trumpet, &c., have been produced without any visible agency.

Fourthly. All the functions of the human body and mind are influenced, in what appear to be certain abnormal states of the system, by causes not yet adequately understood or accounted for. The "occult force" or invisible power, frequently interrupts the normal operation of the faculties, suspending sensation and voluntary motion, and reducing the temperature of the body to a death-like coldness and rigidity; and diseases hitherto considered incurable have been entirely eradicated by this mysterious agency.

The petitioners proceed to state that two opinions prevail with respect to the origin of these phenomena. One ascribes them to the power and intelligence of departed spirits, operating upon the elements which pervade all material forms; the other rejects this conclusion, and contends that all these results may be accounted for in a rational and satisfactory manner.

The memorialists, while thus disagreeing as to the causes, concur in opinion as to the occurrence of the alleged phenomena, and in view of their origin, nature, and bearing upon the interests of mankind, demand for them a patient, rigid, scientific investigation; and request the appointment of a scientific commission for that purpose.

I have now given a faithful synopsis of this petition, which, however unprecedented in itself, has been prepared with singular ability, presenting the subject with great delicacy and moderation. I make it a rule to present any petition to the Senate which is respectful in its terms, upon any subject which the petitioners may desire to bring to the attention of this body. But having discharged this duty I may be permitted to say, that the prevalence of this delusion, at this age of the world, amongst any considerable portion of our citizens, must originate, in my opinion, in a defective system of education, or in a partial derangement of the mental faculties, produced by a diseased condition of the physical organization. I cannot, therefore, believe that it prevails to the extent indicated in this petition. Different ages of the world have had their peculiar delusions. Alchemy occupied the attention of eminent men for several centuries. But there was something sublime in alchemy. The philosopher's stone, or the transmutation of base metals into gold, the *elixir vitae,* or water of life, which would preserve youth and beauty, and prevent old age, decay, and death, were blessings which poor humanity ardently desired, and which alchemy sought to discover by perseverance and piety.

Roger Bacon, one of the greatest alchemists, and greatest men of the thirteenth century, whilst searching for the philosopher's stone, discovered the telescope, burning glasses, and gunpowder. The prosecution of that delusion led, therefore, to a number of useful discoveries. In the sixteenth century, flourished Cornelius Agrippa, alchemist, astrologer, and magician, one of the greatest professors of *hermetic philosophy* that ever lived. He had all the spirits of the air and demons of the earth under his command. Paulus Jovius says "that the devil, in the shape of a large black dog, attended Agrippa wherever he went." Thomas Nash says that "at the request of Lord Surrey, Erasmus, and other learned men, Agrippa called up from the grave several of the great philosophers of antiquity; among others, Tully, whom he caused to redeliver his celebrated oration for Roscius." To please the Emperor, Charles the V., he summoned King David and King Solomon from the tomb, and the emperor conversed with them long upon the science of government. This was a glorious exhibition of spiritual power, compared with the insignificant manifestations of the present day.

I will pass over the celebrated Paracelsus, for the purpose of making allusion to an Englishman, with whose veracious history every one ought to make himself acquainted. In the sixteenth century, Doctor Dee made much progress in the power to hold familiar converse with spirits and angels, and to learn from them all the secrets of the universe . . . The spirits of the olden time were a malignant race, and took especial delight in doing mischief; but the new generation is mild and benignant. These spirits, as this petition attests, indulge in the most innocent amusements and harmless recreations, such as sliding, raising and "tipping" tables, producing pleasant sounds and variegated lights, and sometimes curing diseases which were previously considered incurable; and, for the existence of this simple and benignant race, our petitioners are indebted to the brethren of the Rosie Cross . . .

Mr. Weller. What does the Senator propose to do with the petition?

Mr. Pettit. Let it be referred to three thousand clergymen. [Laughter.]

Mr. Shields. I present the petition.

Mr. Sumner. To what committee is it to be referred?

Mr. Weller. I suggest that it be referred to the Committee on Foreign Relations. [Laughter.]

Mr. Shields. I am willing to agree to that reference.

Mr. Weller. It may be that we may have occasion to enter into diplomatic relations with these spirits. [Laughter.] If so, it is a proper subject for the consideration of that committee. It may be necessary to ascertain whether or not Americans, when they leave this world, lose their citizenship. It may be expedient that all these *grave* questions should be considered by the Committee on Foreign Relations, of which I am an humble member. I move its reference to that committee.

Mr. Mason. I really think it has been made manifest by the honorable Senator who has presented the petition, that he has gone further into the subject than any of us, and that his capacity to elucidate it, is greater than that of any other Senator; I would, therefore, suggest to him that it should either go to a select committee on his motion, or be referred to the Committee on Military Affairs, of which he is chairman. Certainly the Committee on Foreign Relations have nothing to do with it. Perhaps it would be better to allow the petition to lie on the table.

Mr. Shields. This is an important subject, and should not be sneered away in this manner. [Laughter.] I was willing to agree to the motion of the honorable Senator from California; but I do not wish to send the petition to the Committee on Foreign Relations, unless the chairman of that committee is perfectly satisfied that he can do the subject justice. I had thought of proposing to refer the matter to the Committee on the Post Office and Post Roads, because there may be a possibility of establishing a spiritual telegraph between the material and the spiritual world.

Mr. Mason. I move that the petition lie upon the table.

Mr. Shields. I am willing to allow it to lie on the table for the present.

The motion was agreed to; and the petition was ordered to lie on the table.[8]

Since the majority of the members were not willing to finance an investigation into the question of spiritual communication, interested parties in the Congress were obliged to carry on their activities with private funds until more definitive discoveries might alter the disposition of the members of the Senate. The friends of spiritualism watched carefully for some particularly convincing sign that might galvanize public opinion and the Congress into taking direct action—some episode that would dramatize the possibility of establishing a bridge into the land of the dead.[9]

This needed opportunity seemed to be presented in the scheduled execution on Friday the 13th of July, 1860, of the notorious pirate John Hicks on Bedloe's Island in New York harbor. The bloody murders of the pirate and his forthcoming public execution seemed tailor-made for an important experiment. The attractive aspect of the execution from "the scientific point of view"—the probing of the possibility of life after death—arose from the fact that the federal authorities decided to execute the pirate at a public hanging on Bedloe's Island as a stern lesson to other seafaring adventurers who might be tempted to profit from similar acts of piracy. It was felt that if a skilled medium could be present some sign might appear, and if the signal manifested itself in the presence of a multitude it would be difficult for scoffers to gainsay it. Thus, in the interest of science and the spirits persons allied to the cause arranged to have Margaret Fox attend the execution with them to watch for a signal.

The excursion steamship companies and the concessionaires also

---

[8] *Congressional Globe,* Thirty-Third Congress, 1st Session, XXVIII, Part II, 923–924, 1082; for more on congressmen and spirits see Washington *National Intelligencer,* April 19, 21, 28, 1854.

[9] *National Intelligencer,* January 8, 1857.

recognized the unique opportunity presented by the pending execution of the pirate Hicks and for many days before the event steamship companies owning such famous craft as the "commodious" *Red Jacket,* and the "luxurious" *Chicopel* advertised their excursions: "Ho! For the Execution. The beautiful and commodious *Chicopel* will leave this city on Friday morning, for the purpose of affording an opportunity of witnessing the execution of John Hicks, the pirate. This will be a fine chance for all to view the exit of one of these scourges of the seaman's profession. Refreshments on board." [10] Some of the steamship lines were more discreet, merely announcing excursions in the bay and around Bedloe's Island delicately hinting at the event which was to take place under federal auspices.

At nine o'clock on the morning of Friday, July 13th, one of Greeley's editors boarded the official steamer, the *Red Jacket* and noticed a few unidentified congressmen on board, federal marshals Joseph Thompson, Laurence D'Angelis, U. S. Commissioner Stillwell and a large body of reporters; "in addition to these, there were nearly a thousand men well known about town, particularly in the vicinity of City Hall, men who are always seen at public festivals and merrymakings of every kind." A bar was "well stocked with drink and a table piled high with sandwiches."

At nine-thirty John Hicks was brought up from the Tombs to board the steamer to take him to Bedloe's Island where the federal gallows had been erected. Crowds of New Yorkers, unable to take the excursion, lined the streets and collected at the wharfside for a glimpse of the pirate who came aboard dressed in "an inexpensive suit of blue cloth with anchors embroidered upon the white collar. His hands were fastened before him." Except for his handcuffs the pirate was free to walk the decks and to mingle with the excursionists. "His manner was calm and he was apparently without feeling; he certainly showed no emotion, and occasionally came up into the saloon, wearing a smile on his face." He expressed no wish regarding the execution nor any interest in the slight overtures made to him by "scientifically" minded passengers on board. The one detail about which he seemed willing to carry on a

[10] New York *Tribune,* July 14, 1860.

conversation with the passengers who approached him was that the execution "should be conducted as rapidly as possible." He was further "understood to say that he wished no one to speak to him on the gallows except the confessor." Apparently, he had no interest at all in experiments related to spiritualism.

As the *Red Jacket* left the dockside in Manhattan, "the crowd ate, drank, and made merry—a merriment slightly subdued perhaps, but not repressed." On the way the boat took a pleasure trip up the river some distance, and then headed directly to the Island which was reached at eleven o'clock.

After the vessel had been moored to the wharf, Federal Marshal Rynders addressed the large crowd on board requesting all general spectators to disembark and find positions on shore near the gallows in order to view the proceedings. The officials and political dignitaries then arranged themselves in a proper procession for the solemn parade in the great saloon deck of the steamer. And the official party marched four abreast up the hill to the gallows, preceded by a squad of city police.[11]

As Hicks walked from the saloon through the open ranks of this procession to his place at the head, he appeared still unmoved, and it was impossible to say that the paleness of his face was not alone the effect of his confinement. Instead of the hat which he wore when he first came aboard, he had upon his head the black cap soon to be drawn over his face; it was worn rather jauntily, and from its top fluttered streaming ribbons. Upon his shoulders was a silken cape, also black.[12]

The gallows was placed on the northeasterly slope of the island, almost at the water's edge and to lend a federal solemnity to the occasion a company of United States soldiers formed a hollow square about the timber of the scaffolding. As the procession came up, this square was filled with persons who had official status including the "scientific observers," many privileged members of the press, and people from City Hall.

The scene [related Horace Greeley's special observer] was most striking. The brow of the hill was covered with a dense throng of men; in front of

---

[11] *Ibid.*   [12] *Ibid.*

them was the square of the military, including the gallows, beneath which the prisoner and his confessor kneeled on the Greensward; the bay was alive with water-craft of many kinds, including barges in tow, a large number of excursion steamers, and innumerable rowboats, all crowded and sending up shouts and jeers and the hum of a thousand voices. Now and then a white-winged yacht glided past, this also carrying a double freight. The sloop *E. A. Johnson,* the theatre of the crime for which the pirate was to suffer death, was there, gay with flags, filled with friends of the murdered Captain Burr. Over all was the most cheering atmosphere and a flood of sunlight, beneath which the waters sparkled and shone with a joyous brightness, which would give to the saddest misanthrope a new desire to live among men in the world. There was a sublimity in the scene which should have subdued the clamor of the mob to silence; but it was not so. When the prisoner arose from his prayer and stood beneath the rope the people in the boats, thinking that the officials were closing about him to hide the view, raged like wild beasts deprived of their food. They hurled coarse commands to stand aside; they cursed the marshal and the marshal's deputies; they howled as only mobs can howl at individuals whom for the moment they hate.

But soon the rope was adjusted, the officials stood to one side and the great throng could see the object of that morning's drama;

and then for a few seconds, the man for a sight of whose death struggles they cried aloud looked out upon the wonderful picture before him. The shipping, bedecked with flags, was as gay as a Sicilian *fiesta;* there was needed only music to make the occasion perfect, and all this concourse of people, this glitter and array was for Hicks the pirate! It is probable that his thoughts were upon other things, though he seems not to have any above the vanity of desiring to make a brilliant death.

"As the prisoner stood with the rope about his neck and waited for the drawing of the black cap, his eyes again turned toward the sloop, on whose deck he did his frightful murder, now lying almost at his feet.

Hicks had gazed upon it as he ascended the hill. For a second he had seemed to imply to those official and scientific persons who were anxiously watching that he saw the spirit of Captain Burr upon the deck of the sloop, but then his attention had been drawn to the sight of the gallows and his mind and eyes were distracted from the interest which brought the scientific observers to these proceedings.

Hicks, however, at that moment had little time to meditate upon irrelevant matters, for the "final act hastened on, the weight was cut and he was run into the air. There was hardly a motion of a limb, and nothing that could be called a struggle"; and certainly no anticipated sign appeared.

The immense flotilla of small boats then began to break up and spectators began to seek pleasure elsewhere. "The large steamers, rolling heavily by reason of their dangerous loads, went clumsily off." The throng of officials, "scientific persons," and visiting congressmen "returned to the *Red Jacket* and the seductions of the hospitable bar." On the return trip of the steamer to the city, made longer by another cheerful side excursion in the bay, an injudicious congressman called upon the gathering in the saloon bar to express a vocal "thank you" to Federal Marshal Rynders for the efficient manner in which he had dispatched the spirit of the pirate Hicks into the next world, so efficient, indeed, as to escape the watchful eyes of the spectators. Marshal Rynders thanked the gathering for their appreciation of his "painful duty"; but when the crowd "strangely misjudged" his mood and attempted to "give him three cheers," Rynders at once rebuked the saloon crowd and brought the concluding moments of the voyage to a sombre close.[18]

[18] *Ibid.,* for similar and related details see New York *Evening Post,* July 14, 15, 1860; Horace Greeley, Papers, ms.; *United States* v. *Hicks,* ms.; Hamlin Garland, *Forty Years of Psychic Research,* pp. 14–22.

Lincoln and the Spirits

WHEN ABRAHAM LINCOLN came to Washington as President he soon took notice of the widespread interest that many Americans held in spiritualism. In 1861 Robert Dale Owen, a student of and believer in many of the frothy movements of the day, read the President a long paper on spiritualism and related subjects. Lincoln's only comment was "Well, for those who like that sort of thing I should think it is just about the sort of thing they would like." [1] Two years later Senator Edwin D. Morgan wrote Lincoln asking if he would accept as a gift a few books on the subject written by Margaret Fox's friend and admirer, N. P. Tallmadge. Lincoln replied that "the books will be gratefully accepted by me." The noted medium Nettie Colburn Maynard attested to Lincoln's interest in psychic phenomena—particularly clairvoyance— and she often conducted private séances for the President and his wife. While Lincoln dabbled with spiritualism—or tolerated it—there is little

---

[1] Carl Sandburg, *Abraham Lincoln: The War Years,* II, 306.

evidence that he ever took a serious view of the phenomena of the spirit rappers.[2]

Mrs. Lincoln, on the other hand, recently having lost her son Willie, put a higher value upon spirit messages. She told her friend Senator Orville H. Browning on one occasion that she had just been to consult the medium Mrs. Laury who had put her in contact with Willie's spirit. The seeress also made the startling revelation that all the members of Lincoln's cabinet were his enemies and would have to be dismissed if the war were to be won.[3]

Apparently, the President kept his own counsel, and most of his cabinet, despite this warning. And his wife continued to go to the sittings. One night "with eyes smiling" she came to "Emilie's" room in the White House enthralled over news from Willie. "He lives, Emilie!" she cried. "He comes to me every night and stands at the foot of my bed, with the same sweet, adorable smile he always had." [4]

One evening in April of 1863 Lincoln invited the spiritualist medium Charles E. Shockle to stage a sitting at the White House. The President made no secret of the matter. A newspaper correspondent for the Boston *Gazette* was invited as well as Mr. Welles and Mr. Stanton of his cabinet. Presumably, Lincoln wanted some diversion and wished to show Mrs. Lincoln the humorous side of the spirit rappers.

The session began at about eight and was just getting under way when the President was called away. The spirits expressed their pique at having their illustrious guest called away on matters of state by "pinching Mr. Stanton's ears and twitching Mr. Welles' beard." These pranks were made easy by the almost total darkness required for the workings of a spiritualistic séance.

When the President returned serious business was again resumed. Tables moved, raps were heard, and a picture of Henry Clay hanging upon the wall swayed from side to side. Finally, about nine o'clock distinct rappings were heard directly below Lincoln's feet. A delegation of

---

[2] Abraham Lincoln, *The Collected Works of Abraham Lincoln*, VII, 133. See also for interesting material Nettie Colburn Maynard, *Was Abraham Lincoln a Spiritualist?*

[3] Sandburg, *Lincoln: The War Years*, II, 261.

[4] *Ibid*. Emilie was the child's nurse.

American Indians wished to consult with the President. Lincoln said he would be glad to hear from a group of dead Indians because he had occasion not long ago to feel grateful to a delegation of live Indians who visited him, as they were the only delegation he had talked to in a long time "which did not volunteer some advice about the conduct of the war." Unfortunately, the dead Indians were not similarly courteous; they told him that "proclamations were useless; make a bold front and fight the enemy," plus much more uninspiring advice. "That is not Indian talk, Mr. Shockle," remarked the President. In the same manner the advice of Washington, Lafayette, Franklin, and Napoleon was brought forward from the spirits.

"Well," exclaimed the President, "opinions differ among the saints as well as among the sinners. They don't seem to understand running the machines among the celestials much better than we do. Their talk and advice sounds very much like the talk of my cabinet—don't you think so, Mr. Welles?"

Inquiry was made of the spirits as to what could be done to sink the Confederate cruiser *Alabama,* then harassing Union shipping. The spirits replied that the English would soon seize the *Alabama.* Lincoln was amused at this good news, but he told his navy secretary not to leave interception of the *Alabama* solely in the hands of the spirits. "Mr. Welles," Lincoln said, "don't let one gunboat or monitor less be built" even though the celestial aides apparently had found a solution to the vexing problem of the celebrated Confederate cruiser.

Near the end of the session Lincoln told Mr. Shockle that although he had been much entertained he felt that the spirits that night had fallen somewhat short of a celestial stature. The President then expressed a desire to hear a word from Stephen A. Douglas who had passed on two years before.

In this instance the medium chose to go into a trance and thus dispense with the tedious rapping telegraph. Almost at once Mr. Shockle was seized by an unseen force which held him in a state of spiritual rapture. He leaped to his feet, stood up behind his chair "resting his left arm on the back, his right arm thrust into his bosom" as was Douglas' custom. "In a voice such as no one could mistake who had ever heard Mr. Douglas, he spoke. I shall not pretend to quote the language. It was eloquent and choice." The spirit of Lincoln's former colleague from Illinois *via* Mr. Shockle's mediumship gave the President advice on the conduct of the war effort. "The turning-point in this war," said Douglas' spirit, "will be the proper use of victories." Lincoln nodded; he would accept that observation "whether it comes from spirit or human."

At this point, as both Mr. Shockle and Mrs. Lincoln were exhausted, the White House sitting adjourned.[5]

During this period a much more spectacular spiritualist than Mr. Shockle was honoring the city of Washington with his talents. This gentleman, Charles J. Colchester by name, was later to be the central figure in a celebrated spiritualism trial in the federal court at Buffalo, New York—a case in which a federal judge and jury were for a time expected to determine the status of spirits in federal law. The versatile Colchester, who claimed to be the illegitimate son of an English duke "stood the city of Washington upon its ear" during the late 'fifties and early 'sixties. From the green fields of spiritualism which Margaret Fox with the aid of ex-governor Tallmadge and old Waddy Thompson had sown in the city Colchester reaped a big harvest during the first Lincoln administration. He not only won the confidence of the President's wife, but was often summoned for special séances in the White House to amuse and amaze Mr. Lincoln.

Colchester was a stout, well-formed man with an intelligent, aristocratic brow, a bountiful moustache, and a manner befitting the highest British peerage. He created a furore in Washington among the congressmen who, "it was well known," had an "affinity for spirits of all kinds." The medium "had himself drawn on a large wood-cut, with an immense moustache, a high Byronic forehead, and posted over all the fences in Washington." He had an agent, a suite of rooms, and conducted his affairs in a businesslike manner. Colchester claimed to have the power to call up "each man's disembodied relatives." In serious political or military matters he claimed to have a direct line to Julius Caesar. For "women who had lost their blue-eyed children, young men in love, and suspicious gentlemen, who felt their relatives had robbed

[5] Sandburg, *Lincoln: The War Years*, III, 343, 345. Also for related material see Boston *Gazette*, April 23, 1863.

them by faulty wills" Colchester provided a consultative service which harnessed the wisdom of the great men who now reclined in the "Far Beyond." Even "boozy Senators" who wanted to know how to win the next election received sage counsel from Colchester's contacts with the successful politicians of bygone ages.[6]

A journalist attached to the Washington *Star* wrote, some time after Lincoln's death, that he did not "think the fact of Mr. Lincoln being frequently visited by Colchester is any evidence whatever that he was at all inclined to spiritualism." In fact, this writer noted that Colchester himself never associated much with spiritualists and very likely did not believe in its doctrines; but Colchester "had a wonderful gift . . . was one of those $2 fellows—and made money out of it." Everyone who had heard of him wanted to see him, including Mr. Lincoln. He was even more of a sensation in Washington than Margaret Fox had been some years before when it had been rumored that she had held private sessions for Mrs. Franklin Pierce at the White House. "Is it at all strange then that Mr. Lincoln should have had some curiosity to see the man?" asked this writer. Colchester was "continually being sent for by prominent Congressmen to visit their rooms or they called upon him at his rooms." Colchester loved convivial parties. On some occasions, according to this observer, he would walk the streets with his congressional friends frolicking about the town. "At every invitation to a drink he would say that he had to see the spirits about it. Then slapping his hand on a lamp-post" he would secure a response from the spirits saying "yes" or "no."

The correspondent for the *Star* recalled that when one visited Colchester it was the custom to write some twenty questions upon different sheets of paper folding each separately and then placing them on a table. The medium would write an answer to each question. "He wrote very rapidly; and as fast as he wrote an answer he, without hesitation, picked out the question to which it was a response, and at times he was surprisingly correct. . . . I could never comprehend it . . . and I had two witnesses with me both times." [7]

[6] New York *Tribune*, August 25, 1865; for some related material see Hamlin Garland, *Forty Years of Psychic Research*, pp. 14–15.

[7] Washington *Star* quoted and referred to in the New York *Tribune*, August 25,

Noah Brooks, Horace Greeley's Washington correspondent, claimed that he caught Colchester red-handed in a "fraud" which certainly was no surprise. On the basis of this contention Brooks said that he was called to the White House to confront Colchester with these facts. Brooks claimed that in the presence of Mrs. Lincoln he called the medium "a swindler and a humbug" and told him to "get out of this house and out of this city at once. If you are in Washington tomorrow afternoon at this time you will be in Old Capitol prison . . . The little scamp . . . sneaked out of the house and I never saw or heard of him afterward." Noah Brooks' story does not coincide with the facts. Colchester was not a "little scamp." He may have been a scamp but he was not little; he was a man of extraordinary physical size. It is strange that Brooks never heard of him afterward since Colchester was the central figure in the famous "spiritualism trial" which took place a few months later in Buffalo and was copiously reported in Greeley's paper.[8] The facts would seem to be that Lincoln enjoyed Colchester's great showmanship, while Mrs. Lincoln took the medium more seriously.

Some time later, on February 4, 1872, seven years after the assassination of the President, Mrs. Lincoln visited Boston and "incognito and closely veiled attended a public seance of a well known lady medium [Margaret Fox] on Washington Street." At first Mrs. Lincoln attempted to keep her identity a secret, but a few days later she registered at Park's House under the name of "Mrs. Linder" and remained there for ten days, during which she made frequent visits to Margaret Fox. Persons in Boston who knew Mrs. Lincoln reported that the dead President's widow believed that through Margaret Fox she had been in actual contact with "the real presence of the spirit of her husband." [9]

1865. For other examples of the same type of story see New York *Times*, August 27, 30, September 1, 3, 22, 30, 1865, Buffalo *Express*, August 21, 1865 and John Worth Edmonds, "Judge Edmonds on 'Spiritualism'," *Nation*, I (September 7, 1865), 295–296.

[8] Sandburg, *Lincoln: The War Years*, III, 346.

[9] New York *Times*, February 24, 1872. For a related story see Boston *Herald*, February 20, 1872.

Spirits in the Courts

FOR SEVERAL YEARS following the rise of Margaret Fox, practical persons had looked forward to the possibility that a medium might some day be forced to present proof before a court of law to support asserted claims of a contact with another world. Two spectacular law cases of this nature finally occurred shortly after the Civil War: *Muller* v. *New York State* and *Colchester* v. *United States.*

The first of these two cases involved William H. Muller and William W. Silver who operated a photography gallery at Number 630 Broadway. These two remarkable artist-chemists claimed to be able to take pictures of the spirits of persons who had passed on from the physical world into the world beyond. Various members of the clergy in the city of New York, opposing this invasion of their domains, requested the police to look into the fraud which they said was being daily perpetrated by Muller and Silver. As a result, a resourceful police inspector tricked the photographers into developing a spirit-picture of a former mayor of the city who, unfortunately for Muller and Silver, was still alive even though the inspector had requested the photograph under the pretense that his honor was among the blessed ones no longer in the mortal world.

Armed with this material evidence of fraud perpetrated by the spirit-photographers the police inspector took the two artists down to the Tombs and lodged them in jail to await trial.

Muller and Silver protested that it was no fault of theirs that the spirit of the ex-mayor, even though he was still alive, found its way into the lens and chemicals of their photographic apparatus. Their duty was not to answer for the causes of these miracles, but rather to act as intermediaries between this world and the next. Justice James Dowling, who had been responsible for having the two photographers arraigned for an examination before the law, was besieged with letters and threats from spiritualists who warned him of the grave danger inherent in abusing two chemists who had been assigned to perform a great duty by the powers that be.

On the morning of April 24, 1869 in Justice Dowling's Court of New York City a large crowd was on hand to hear several learned counselors debate the issue of whether the photographs were miracles or frauds. The state's attorney Elbridge Gerry led the prosecution and the famed lawyer, John T. Townsend, was at hand for the defense.[1]

The state's attorney presented the facts of the situation to the courts, adding for good measure that this case afforded an opportunity to strike down the insanity of spiritualism which was abroad in the land.

Under the guiding hand of defense attorney Townsend, Muller presented his defense. The photographer testified that his system of chemical contact with the spirit world was still in its infancy, just as the signals which Morse was at first able to generate were mere trifles when compared to the modern telegraph. Muller pleaded for more time to perfect this wonderful new contact with the spirit world. The attorney for the defense excoriated the state's attorney for calling spiritualists insane. "There are eleven million spiritualists in the United States; they can't all be insane," he shouted. Townsend likened Muller to Bacon and Galileo. He warned the judge that history was being made that day in

---

[1] New York *Times,* April 13, 1869.

his court. Townsend insisted that it was not Muller alone who was on trial but the eleven million spiritualistic believers in the United States were sitting with Mr. Muller in the docket.

In rebuttal, state's attorney Gerry called the respected "humbug artist" P. T. Barnum to the stand to assert that, in his expert opinion, Muller's pretensions were pure fraud. Gerry then acknowledged the eloquence of Townsend's plea, but insisted that he was not "prosecuting the spiritualists, but only Muller as a fraud." Even if Muller believed that he was engaged in a divine chemistry his art was still a fraud, insisted Gerry; and in any case, he told the court, it was imperative that the court brand Muller's "art" as a fraud since the acceptance of it presented a threat to the very existence of the Christian religion. Spiritualism, he warned the court, was only a "revival of ancient Pantheism"; he cited innumerable ancient hallucinations and then concluded with the assertion that spirit-photography was but one more hallucination or more likely it was only a plain fraud.[2]

At the close of the proceedings Judge Dowling took the matter aside to his chamber for study and then ruled that "after a careful and thorough analysis of this interesting and extraordinary case" he had come to the conclusion that he must dismiss the case, as the state had failed to prove that Muller's pictures were a fraud.[3]

The more spectacular of the two law cases which attempted to test the validity of spiritualistic claims involved the extravagant assertions of the convivial Charles J. Colchester who had brought amusement to Lincoln and, perhaps, some consternation to the President's wife. At the end of the war Colchester had moved his operations from Washington to the city of Buffalo. This change proved to be a serious error on the part of the "illegitimate British peer." In the city of Washington he had been free to display his wonders immune from legal harassment because of his great popularity among the members of Congress, but when he began to practice his art in Buffalo, religious groups in that city suggested that law-enforcement officers might well test the possibility of forcing spiritualistic mediums to comply with the federal tax law which at that time required sleight-of-hand artists to secure a

2 *Ibid.*, April 21, 1869.
3 *Ibid.*, May 4, 1869.

license in order to practice their profession. The "peerage" in Colchester's character forced him to refuse to demean himself by the payment of a juggler's tax claiming the constitutional privilege customarily granted the clergy. The federal marshal met this defiance with an arrest and as a result Colchester was forced to appear before the federal district court in Buffalo in order to determine whether he was a member of the clergy or a practitioner of the art of jugglery.[4]

Nonspiritualists were very pleased at this turn of events as they saw an opportunity to test the validity of spiritualistic claims in a federal court. The followers of spiritualism rallied to lend their persecuted colleague moral support. The Colchester case at once became a celebrated issue which received columns of comment in the metropolitan press. Correspondents rushed to Buffalo with the same urgency that brought newsmen to Dayton, Tennessee many decades later.

Greeley, having by this time lost his faith in the cause, directed his paper to assume that at long last the issue would be settled. The *Herald* took up its old wolf cry against the spirits and Raymond of the *Times*, assuming a judicial attitude in long editorials, asserted that "the merely material phenomena of spiritualism, as attested by thousands of intelligent witnesses, under circumstances which preclude the possibility of deception, are such as cannot be invalidated by the verdict of a jury in an isolated case." There was much in these phenomena, said Raymond, "worthy of the candid attention of the curious and the thoughtful." The progress of the spiritualistic faith, "the numbers and character of the believers, and the sacred claims set up for it, as comforter of the sorrowing and the guide to the doubtful, remove it merely from the category of the mischievous humbugs." He saw its abuses and he wondered if these might not be explained by the spiritualist theory that "there are both good and bad spirits, the latter ever trying to lead us astray." While being kind to the sincere spiritualists, the editor spent his wrath upon the "paid and peddling mediums who by reasons of their sordid interest in peculiarly marvellous manifestations are tempted to deceive." In this editorial the great Raymond of the *Times* was rea-

---

[4] Buffalo *Courier*, September 1, 1865; the same story in general terms may be found in New York *Tribune*, August 25, 1865.

soning along lines very similar to that of the spiritualists, but a few
weeks later he had changed his mind.[5]

The Colchester case opened in the United States District Court at
Buffalo on Saturday morning, August 19, 1865. The courtroom was
packed with spectators who had arrived early to witness this novel case.
The defense attorneys, Messrs. Cook and Hibbard, moved for a dismissal on the grounds that the license law could not be applied to the
spiritualistic activities of Colchester, since to do so would violate the
provision of the Constitution providing that "Congress shall make no
law respecting the establishment of religion or the provision of the free
exercise thereof." This motion being denied, a jury was impaneled,
and the case moved forward.

The prisoner at the bar [said the prosecutor] stands indicted for the
offense of practicing the trade or profession of a juggler, without having
procured a license . . . [His] performance of singular and extraordinary
feats of rappings, answering questions enclosed in envelopes . . . will not be
seriously contested, perhaps admitted . . .

I see assembled here a great multitude, not "the spirits of men" but men
and women in corporeal frame. While I concede the inestimable value of
the press, I cannot forbear the remark that it has been made the instrument
of magnifying this case into undue proportions, and to cause the public to
believe that this case is a contest between the United States and a large
body of citizens calling themselves Spiritualists, and an endeavor on the
part of the United States to crush out a religious sect and to expose its
heresies if it has any, and that the result of this trial will establish the fact
of whether Spiritualism is true or false. Nothing could be further from the
truth.

The result of this trial [said the federal attorney] can establish no such
thing. It is a simple inquiry whether Charles J. Colchester is practicing
sleight of hand under the guise of spiritual control. I trust, therefore, should
there be a believer in this faith upon the jury he will not look upon me as a
persecutor, but will go hand in hand with me in my endeavor to expose
the defendant's impositions if he is an imposter, and to compel him, if he
is a juggler, to contribute his proportion to the government.[6]

The prosecutor then attempted to establish through the testimony

---

[5] New York *Times,* September 1, 1865.   [6] *Ibid.*

of Jake Rogers, John H. Anderson, and John M. McCallister, all former associates of Colchester, that the medium had taught all of these persons the tricks of his profession. "There are and ever have been," said the federal attorney, "tricks in what used to be known as the black arts—a jugglery—" which have always baffled interpretation and examination.

On cross examination, Defense Attorney Cook challenged the prosecution's witnesses, who claimed Colchester had taught them his "black art," to perform one of Colchester's feats for the court. The defense attorney wrote a man's name upon a piece of paper, folded it, and then placed the paper upon the jury bar at the same time challenging the witness against Colchester to identify the name—a feat which the defendant had performed hundreds of times. The witness refused the challenge. Another witness had testified that Colchester had taught him how to produce blood-writing on his arm. When challenged by the defense to reproduce this black art before the court this witness also was unable to give a demonstration of the lessons he said he had learned from Colchester.[7]

After the prosecution had employed several days of testimony in the presentation of its case Attorney Hibbard took over for the defense. The first witness called was Judge J. C. Chumesero of Monroe County New York. This jurist testified that in the company of his friend A. M. Jones of Rochester he had visited Colchester's studio in Rochester and witnessed the defendant's remarkable feats of blood-writing and ancestor identification; he was convinced, he said, that Colchester undoubtedly possessed supernatural powers. The prosecution was unable to upset Judge Chumesero's testimony during cross-examination. Thomas Kean and other journalists working for the Buffalo *Courier* were then called as witnesses and all testified that they had often visited Colchester's performances but were unable to fathom how he managed his alleged miracles.[8]

In the rebuttal the federal prosecuting attorney challenged Colchester to perform a miracle in the court, to demonstrate whether he was priest or practitioner of a black art. When the baronial medium

[7] New York *Times,* September 1, 1865.
[8] *Ibid.,* September 3, 22, 27, 1865.

disdainfully refused to demean his "God-given" communicability in such degrading and compulsory circumstances the prosecutor asked the jury to draw its own conclusions. Finally, after days of testimony the jury returned a verdict against Colchester and Judge Hall fined the medium 40 dollars plus 473 dollars in costs. The defense entered a motion for a new trial which was refused a few days later by the judge, at which time the jurist rendered an opinion of significance.[9]

Judge Hall said that he denied the motion for a new trial because Colchester had failed to present a logical defense. Since the medium asked the jury to accept as true claims which were contrary to accepted standards of reason, the burden of proof, in logic if not in law, rested upon the defendant. Strong proof of the claims of spiritualism were therefore required, but instead of proofs, said Judge Hall, the defendant had failed to demonstrate even his lesser skills when "their exercise would have been more profitable to him than all his exhibitions could be" and even more conclusive, said the jurist, was the fact that among the hundreds of mediums in America not one could be found who would embrace this "opportunity to prove upon a judicial trial the sincerity and truth of their pretensions, if such could be made." [10]

The night following the reports of the Colchester decision a mass meeting of spiritualists "composed mostly of progressive gentlemen of venerable aspect" gathered at Metropolitan Hall in New York City to protest against Judge Hall's decision. After some deliberation the gathering decided to form itself into a "Religio-Political Court of the People" and retry the case in a new light. Colonel John Goodwin was appointed judge; Colonel Tom Picton acted as counsel for Colchester, who was absent; an anonymous gentleman assumed responsibility of presenting the case against spiritualism; and the audience took the role of the jury. It was stated that the case was to be heard in a logical manner; "we do not want to be governed by Blackstone or Kent," said Judge Goodwin; the aim of the court was to "avoid legal quibbles and get at the truth."

When it became clear that the jury had no sympathy with anything

---

[9] *Ibid.*, September 30, 1865; for the same story in other sources see Buffalo *Courier*, August 27, September 1, 1865.

[10] Buffalo *Courier*, September 21, 1865.

the unnamed gentleman had to say which might in any way associate Colchester with jugglery it was declared by acclamation that Judge Hall's decision was there and then overturned by this "Religio-Political" tribunal of the people.[11]

The press of the time printed long commentaries evaluating Judge Hall's decision. James Gordon Bennett and Judge Edmonds engaged in a running debate on spiritualism in the pages of the *Herald* which were embellished by Godkin's rasping commentary in the *Nation*.

In angry tones Raymond of the *Times* entered the discussion:

It is no part of our responsibility to pronounce upon the verdict of the jury. Much of the testimony would seem to show that in the judgment of intelligent witnesses some, at least, of Colchester's performances were entirely inexplicable on the hypothesis of "prestidigitation"; and yet if the somewhat unsatisfactory statements of Rogers, the traveling agent of the "Wizard" Anderson are to be accepted, Colchester by his own confession is a mountebank and imposter.

There is much in the phenomena of modern spiritualism, whether as owing to the illustrious origin they claim, or as indicating as yet undiscovered natural laws, or as embodying the latest achievements in the science and art of "humbug," that is well worth the attention of the curious and thoughtful. Few have any conception of the extent to which the investigation of these facts, in private ways, is being conducted. The operations of public, paid "mediums" are but straws on the surface of the vast ocean of popular interest, which this assumed revelation has set in motion. In hundreds of thousands of families, at countless firesides, where imposture would be sacrilege, and in circles of mutually cherished and trusted relatives and friends, between whom the ideas of deception would be even stranger than the facts we are asked to believe, spiritualism is undergoing the test of daily experiments . . .

Certain appearances there are, which, in the judgment of an immense number of people, cannot be explained by the theory of jugglery or any kind of imposture, and so, what is facetiously termed the "investigation" goes on, seldom, we fear, to any good purpose; often, we know to very great harm . . . We have known very respectable people who disgraced themselves by persecuting faithful and innocent servants with charges of theft,

[11] New York *Tribune*, September 1, 1865; see also follow-up story in the New York *Tribune* for September 7, 1865.

on no other authority than that some irresponsible, disembodied vagabond loafing about on the confines of the invisible world. We know a lady, whose personal qualities, position in society, and reputation for common sense, have been of the very highest, and yet who has recently abandoned half of her best friends, because a babbling "medium" pretended to let in light upon their true characters and make revelations about their secret lives. Spirits pretend to point out "true affinities" and make trouble between husband and wife; spirits present new views about right and wrong, remove conscientious scruples by lifting the favored devotee to a higher plane of vision and explode antiquated superstitions, which old-time, bleareyed theologies have dignified with the name of faiths and duties. In short, there is no mischief, whether in the realm of business, love, friendship or religion that some of these spirits are not competent to do, and are not daily doing.

Now, whatever may be said of the existence and influence of "guardian spirits" that minister to our good, here, at least is unmistakable indication of Satanic agency. These are not "spirits of health," but goblins of the damned; bringing with them not "airs from heaven," but "blasts from hell."

The practical inference from all this would seem to be, first—however puzzled you may be with spiritualism, however interested in it as a curious development in philosophy, don't *trust* it; by its own showing it is not a thing to be trusted. Secondly, do not spend much of your time with it unless you are consciously the very man or woman whose mission, clearly indicated by nature and education it is, to study it in the interest of science and religion, truth and humanity.

Who cares, then, if such fellows as Colchester are pronounced by juries to be jugglers? Who cares if they are compelled to pay part of their badly-earned gain for licenses that are required of other mountebanks? Who will not rejoice if the result of such verdicts be to make the profession of "spiritual medium" as unprofitable as it is disreputable, and to destroy a trade which thrives best where human nature is the weakest, and adds nothing to the material, mental or moral wealth of the community in which it is tolerated? [12]

[12] New York *Times,* September 27, 1865.

Spirits in the City of Brotherly Love

FROM THE TIME IN 1852 when Margaret Fox first introduced the visitors from "Summer Land" to the hospitable city of brotherly love, spirits were always welcome in Philadelphia. Certainly, the most remarkable spirit to arrive in the city was one which allegedly belonged to Katie King who had lived in England during the late 1600's.

Katie was the daughter of James King, later knighted by Charles II as Sir John Morgan, sometimes known to the seafaring trade as "the pirate Morgan." The interesting element about Katie King was not her paternity, but the fact that, although she had been dead for over two hundred years, she was now being rematerialized almost nightly in the spring of 1874 by the mediums Mr. and Mrs. Holmes in a studio parlor at Number 50 North Ninth Street in Philadelphia. Katie King's spirit had first appeared in this world a few months previously in London, but her mediums transferred their affairs to Philadelphia in search of a more friendly atmosphere for rematerialization of their subject.

The fact that well known citizens such as Dr. Henry T. Child, Robert Dale Owen, Henry Seybert, and several committees of faculty members from the University of Pennsylvania were nightly holding Katie's hands and conversing in a most familiar way with the reincarnation of this "charming" young person who had died two centuries before aroused considerable comment in the city and some questioning of the actual validity of many of the assertions made by respectable persons who had been privileged to view the proceedings.

Henry J. Raymond hurriedly sent an editor to Philadelphia to cover this event and after several visits to Katie King's surroundings he asserted that, in his opinion, Katie was "one part spiritualism and two parts humbug," but that "her noble army of followers which numbered several hundreds" firmly believed that Katie was walking proof of life after death. The editor of the New York *Times* wrote the following narrative concerning the return of Katie King to the land of the living.

There was no furor about the business; no hall was taken or public entertainment given; but the medium's narrow sitting-room, at No. 50 North Ninth street, was crowded nightly, and sometimes twice of an evening, at a dollar a head, and this, too, in spite of the fact that the public was not only not invited, but not admitted. Only those who could present good testimonials, or were introduced by mutual friends, could gain admission. Among these was your correspondent, who paid his dollar like the rest, and, therefore, feels at liberty to tell all he knows. The house is an old-fashioned, three-story brick, occupied, as to its first floor, by a music store, and as to the rest of it by the Holmes family and the spirits. The *seances* are held in the second story front room, an ordinary apartment, perhaps 18 feet wide by 16 deep, with two windows looking out on Ninth street, and with nothing uncanny about it except the "cabinet," which is made by stretching a dark partition across one corner, thus cutting off a triangular space. The partition reaches to the ceiling, and contains a small door, with a threshold about six inches high. Over the door and about seven feet from the floor is a small pentagonal opening, while another of similar shape but larger size is about a foot lower on the right. This is the aperture at which Katie usually appears. It is about a foot in greatest width and height. The cabinet is hung with loose, dark curtains, and a door at one side, leading to a back room, is boarded over in a manner apparently secure. The audience sits in semicircles facing the cabinet, the inner circle being composed of the most faithful spiritualists. On one end of this row sits the principal medium,

Mrs. Holmes, her husband sometimes taking a chair at the other end, sometimes entering the cabinet and going into a "mesmeric sleep." When your correspondent was present, both mediums remained in full view of the audience during the entire performance. They did not go into a trance, but sat fanning themselves, and laughed and joked like ordinary mortals. One window was closed and darkened and the other remained open. The door was locked and the room dimly illuminated by a coal-oil lamp, with a red shade, which threw upon the scene that roseate tinge so much affected in the spectacular drama. The company being seated, without joining hands, the spirits were invoked through the agency of a small music-box; and when this did not seem to "fetch 'em," the audience sang some familiar melody. It did not appear to matter much what the melody was—sacred or secular, it was all one to them, and they passed from one to the other with the greatest readiness. The only requisite seems to be that the melody should be in a minor key, and tolerably loud. "The better," said some skeptic, "to conceal the creaking of invisible machinery."

After a short overture conducted in this way, Katie appears at the little window above mentioned. She usually begins by thrusting out a white and shapely arm, speedily followed by a pretty face, framed in a mass of black ringlets, and set off by a jaunty Spanish veil, which lies lightly on her head. There is profound silence until she says in a ghostly whisper, "Good evening." The salutation is courteously returned, and then ensues a brisk dialogue of the smallest kind of small talk, interrupted by frequent disappearances and reappearances on the part of the young lady. The tenor of this important communication from the land of the hereafter is about as follows:

"Good evening, Katie."

"Good evening."

"Are you alone this evening?"

"No. Father is here and Gen. Rawlings; but they can't materialize tonight."

"Katie, Mr. Owen (Robert Dale Owen) is here, don't you want to speak to him?"

"Why, of course, stoopid—Good evening, Father Owen."

Mr. Owen bows, and says: "Will you have this bouquet, Katie?"

"Of course I will," says Katie, and reaches her hand for it. It is given her and she disappears with it, but presently returns and gives it to somebody to hold for her.

"Katie, can you come out for us to-night?"

"I'll try, but it's very warm and very hard to materialize."

Katie accordingly disappears, and the singing is resumed. Presently the door of the cabin opens slowly. I sat directly opposite the opening, but could see nothing until it was well ajar; then a white figure seemed to grow out of the darkness within, and Katie stepped forward gracefully, took two or three steps into the room, and retired, closing the door after her by lifting her hand to the latch. She was dressed in a somewhat theatrical costume of pure white, which flowed to her feet and seemed to be of a fine kind of muslin. The sleeves were loose and flowing, and as she waved her hands in the stereotyped style of the stage sylph, the sleeves fell away to the shoulder, displaying a pair of perfect arms which might well arouse the envy of any earthly belle. Her figure was full and round and her face was beautiful in outline and expression with a complexion so clear and transparent that it either seemed to, or actually did, shine with a mild radiance. In her hand she held a fresh bouquet, and a dagger-fan given her at some former *seance* was stuck in her girdle, while on her neck sparkled a silver cross, also a present, suspended from what was said to be a necklace of diamonds. She came and went several times, touching with her hand a number of the audience—among them your correspondent. It was the soft, gentle, magnetic touch of a woman; but the hand that gave it was cool and dry, notwithstanding the furnace-like heat of that closed cabinet. She reclaimed her bouquet, kissed a young lady who was one of her dearest followers, and on one occasion seated herself, with much apparent difficulty, and remained for some moments in full view of the audience.

But the most wonderful part was still to come. "Katie," said Mrs. Holmes, "can you disappear with the door open tonight?" "I'll try," said Katie; and presently she came again, and while the door stood wide open she gradually faded away, seeming to retire slowly into the depths of a space only just large enough to hold her at the first. The bouquets, and all other material substances about her, disappeared at the same time, and when nothing was left but the hem of her white dress shimmering on the floor, she came again, seeming to gather herself from thin air, and to grow, like a forming cloud, more and more distinct, until she again stood in mortal guise before a delighted audience.

Naturally, you will ask for the solution of the mystery. I have none to give. There are, or seems to be, a solid floor beneath, a solid ceiling above, a solid wall on one side, a solidly-closed door on the other. Skeptics have taken the cabinet to pieces; committees, including some of the Faculty of the University of Pennsylvania, have investigated in every way: one would think that no mortal could disappear, even through an acknowledged opening, as readily as Katie King does, without being seen by some of the audience, gazing, as they do, point blank through the open door; both mediums are ignorant people, of low ideas and seemingly of quite too little intelligence to play a trick as delicate as this, and yet this counterfeit presentment is a wonderfully accurate imitation of flesh and blood, and I'll vow that the bouquet of flowers and the brown paper wrapped round their stems came from no heavenly green-house and grocery, and in spite of the music and of Mrs. Holmes' sudden cough, we did hear what sounded very like the creaking of secret machinery on two occasions, and we did see, last Saturday night, the petals of flowers lying in the hall and on the third-story stairs, and the petals were wonderfully like those which adorned a huge bouquet which was that evening handed to Katie King, and disappeared with her. It may be that this is all right. It may be that the noise of the machinery was only the groaning of John King's guilty conscience. It may be that Katie chose to take her return flight by way of the attic stairs and the trap-door in the roof. It may be that we have been entertaining and entertained by angels unawares. But if it is so, if spirits may revisit earth only to talk nonsense, if they can do nothing but prattle and look pretty, and can impart no information of man's state, either present or future, then it seems to me that Spiritualism is a fraud of the biggest kind, and that the spirits would do much better to stay at home and let us form for ourselves other views of the hereafter than that which must regard it as simply an asylum for feeble-minded ghosts.[1]

Mr. F. J. Lippitt, a more sympathetic observer, was charmed by the sprightly and attractive face of Katie King. At times she engaged in brief conversations with Mr. Lippitt during which she occasionally withdrew for a few moments, and presently appeared again. Sometimes she repeatedly called her visitors "stupid," smiling mischievously, and putting up her chin whenever she said this or anything else amusing. It often happened that Katie was unable to accomplish a complete materialization. On these occasions only a part of her would be exhibited through the cabinet window. At the request of Dr. John Child, Katie was once asked to expose her entire arm. Graciously, she repeat-

[1] New York *Times*, July 21, 1874.

edly showed her entire arm bare to the shoulder, putting it entirely out of the window. An involuntary murmur of admiration greeted this exhibition, for the arm was a perfect model for a sculptor, cast in one of nature's finest molds, gracefully rounded, dazzlingly white, but yet of the whiteness of flesh, not of marble. At the Doctor's request she allowed several visitors to go up to the window to feel her hand. Mr. Lippitt placed his hand in Katie's on this occasion. "It was a perfectly natural feminine hand of solid flesh and blood and of a pleasant warmth," said Mr. Lippitt. Even so, he left convinced that Katie was not a living human being.[2]

As the fall season of 1874 opened in Benjamin Franklin's city the mediums Mr. and Mrs. Holmes returned to Philadelphia from their summer holidays and made arrangements once more to present the spirit of Katie King. During that summer, however, young Katie had been unfortunately reprimanded by her fellow residents in "Summer Land" for too great a physical exposure of her being in the real world. A well authenticated report in the press stated that other spirits were prepared to call down on Katie's luckless head a torrent of condemnation if she continued to expose her being so grossly in the future.[3] As a result of these reproaches it was decided in the fall season of 1874, that Katie would materialize only her arms and now and then her face to public view. But even this scant performance was enough to excite the interest of hundreds, including a scientist on the faculty of the University of Pennsylvania "whose name, were it given, would be recognized by hundreds of persons in Philadelphia's best society." [4] As the season progressed articles appeared in periodicals such as the *Atlantic Monthly* and the *Galaxy* which seriously considered the possibility of whether or not Katie King would eventually prove to be the actual beginning of the revelations for which the world had waited centuries.[5]

The Katie King exhibitions during the fall were very successful.

[2] F. J. Lippitt, "Was It Katie King?" *Galaxy*, XVIII (December, 1874), 754–766.
[3] New York *Times*, October 24, 1874.
[4] *Ibid.*
[5] Robert Dale Owen, "How I Came to Study Spiritual Phenomena," *Atlantic Monthly*, XXXIV (November, 1874), 578–590; for additional information see F. J. Lippitt, "Was It Katie King?" *Galaxy*, XVIII (December, 1874), 754–766.

"Things were going smoothly; money was flowing into the coffers of the mediums and Katie's friends were jubilant at the number of converts daily being made to the cause of Spirit materialization," wrote one observer.[6]

Katie might well have been a very great success if it had not been for the prying skepticism of an editor-writer for the Philadelphia *Inquirer*. This cynic made a careful survey of the more luxurious boarding houses in Philadelphia and as a result he found a young woman who very much resembled Katie King. After shadowing the young lady for several evenings as she left her lodgings he found that she always had the Holmes' studio as her destination. Next, this unprincipled young journalist managed to strike up an acquaintance with the young lady who resembled Katie King and was eventually invited to her lodgings in the boarding house where he saw a table filled with gifts which the followers of Katie King had given her including those from Henry Seybert, Professor Robert Hare, Dr. Henry T. Child, and Robert Dale Owen.

The cynic from the *Inquirer* and his publishers then arranged a dramatic exposé in which they confronted several illustrious Philadelphians with the fact that the gifts which they supposed they had given to the Immortal Katie King were actually in the possession of a youthful widow, mother of a young child, who lived in a well known boarding house in the city. The deluded donors were confronted with the fact that Katie was not a materialized spirit, but very much a physical organism who confessed her sins and explained that she had cooperated with the mediums in perpetrating the fraud only as a means to support her child and an aged mother.[7]

A short while after the Katie King episode Margaret Fox was invited to return to Philadelphia, the scene of some of her early successes. Henry Seybert, a wealthy, aristocratic Philadelphian, active member of the Philosophical Society, and trustee of the University of Pennsylvania, desired to investigate spiritualism. Seybert bought a fine

[6] Philadelphia *Inquirer*, December 15, 1874.

[7] *Ibid.*, December 16, 1874; for other interesting stories on Katie King see the *Inquirer* for December 17, 18, 1874, and the Philadelphia *Press* of December 18, 19, 1874.

home in the city which he named "Spiritual Mansion" and he induced
Margaret to come to the city and establish herself as the "high-priestess
of this new temple of unseen entities." Her salary was most liberal and
her situation there was one which would easily have met the wishes
of many ambitious mediums. Margaret hoped that the quiet existence
there would be preferable to the daily and distasteful practice of public
mediumship.

During her stay as resident-medium at the Spiritual Mansion, Margaret delivered messages from departed friends of her patron, and
telegraphed rappings from famous ancient sages and from a few of
the minor saints of the church, but when it appeared that she was required to make contact with members of the twelve apostles, of St. Paul,
Elijah, and the Angel Gabriel, Margaret's rapping telegraph mechanism failed to generate enough magnetism to reach these exalted personages. She told her patron that she considered it an actual sacrilege
even to attempt such a transmission. Margaret confided later to friend
Reuben Davenport that "Henry Seybert had an undoubted vein of madness in his brain." He was, despite these shortcomings, a sincere man
who believed that he was near the threshold of a great discovery. While
there, Margaret told her patron that she made no claim to spiritual
power, but she did not disclose to him the secret of her rapping. Because
of unpleasant scenes arising from her refusal to cooperate, she soon left
Seybert's mansion and returned to New York.[8]

A few months after Seybert's death in 1883 it was learned that he
left sixty-thousand dollars to the University of Pennsylvania to establish a chair in philosophy provided the trustees would also accept an
additional sum to establish a commission to investigate "all systems
which assume to represent the truth; and particularly of modern Spiritualism." This legacy resulted in the celebrated Seybert Commission of
the University in 1884, which included such prominent persons as
S. Weir Mitchell, William Pepper, and Howard H. Furness who served
as chairman. The members of the commission wrote to Margaret Fox
asking her to give them an opportunity to investigate her rappings and

[8] New York *Herald*, September 21, 1888; for a related story see Henry Spicer,
"Spiritual Manifestations," *Littell's Living Age*, 2nd Series, I (June, 1853),
807–820.

as a result the medium became the house guest of Mr. Furness for several days. On the evening of November 5, 1884, Dr. William Pepper, Dr. Joseph Leidy, Dr. George A. Koeing, Professor Robert Ellis Thompson, George S. Fullerton, and Mr. Furness began a series of sittings to investigate Margaret's rapping phenomenon.

The medium told the commissioners that, while she made no claim to extraordinary powers, she would demonstrate, as she had done hundreds of times before, the strange sounds that had so long been associated with her mediumship. The commissioners' sessions with Margaret eventually finished on an indefinite note. While they were certain that the sounds were of a strictly physiological origin and not supernatural, the members were at a loss to discover the source of the rappings except that the noises came from the vicinity of the medium.[9]

A short while later Margaret Fox expressed amusement to her friend Reuben Davenport "over the manner in which she eluded the inquisitions of the grave and conscientious commissioners and left them puzzled over the rappings."[10]

After the medium had gone, the grave and serious gentlemen from the University of Pennsylvania consulted among themselves for several days. Doubts assailed them regarding Margaret Fox. They were of the opinion that the alleged raps might emanate from her person by purely involuntary causes, but the meaning of this hypothesis they scarcely chose to evaluate. Harboring these doubts the gentlemen wrote Margaret again requesting a further searching investigation. The medium replied in a somewhat facetious tone that she agreed with the conclusions of the commission which doubted the supernatural origin of the noises, reminding them that she held the same opinion. Pleading ill health and asserting that nothing new could be learned from a repetition of the sittings Margaret respectfully declined to comply with the second request.[11]

Henry J. Raymond of the New York *Times,* always rankled by the

[9] Davenport, *Death-Blow,* pp. 35–36, 164–167.
[10] *Ibid.,* 201–205.
[11] Pennsylvania University, *Seybert Commission for Investigating Modern Spiritualism. Preliminary Report of the Commission Appointed by the University of Pennsylvania to Investigate Modern Spiritualism in Accordance with the Request of the Late Henry Seybert,* pp. 33–48.

credulity of the general public in America, was particularly disturbed to note that an intelligent city like Philadelphia could produce such incidents as Katie King and Seybert's Spiritual Mansion. It seemed, said Raymond, that the citizens of Benjamin Franklin's city, having "cut themselves adrift from the faith of the Christian religion, have no other resource but some strange delusion." [12]

[12] New York *Times,* February 14, 1886.

Ghosts from Coast to Coast

THE "TOWERING FANTASY" nourished by Margaret Fox and her imitators continued to spread from coast to coast. It became so commonplace that by the 'seventies and 'eighties the Boston spiritualists—to cite a good example—were a rather jaded lot. Simple sensations like rapping or table tilting were not sufficient to attract public attention and the spirits hovering in the atmosphere about the intellectually hallowed streets of Boston had to endow their chosen mediums with extraordinary devices in order to capture the attention of the late-nineteenth-century Bostonians.[1]

One device the spirits employed to awaken interest was a process called "materialization," by which a spirit appeared in the flesh. E. L. Godkin, publisher of the *Nation*, having sent a correspondent to investigate the impact of this "diabolistic" device upon intellectual Boston, reported that the activity of the spiritualists rivaled that of other religious sects in the city. The audiences of Boston mediums were necessarily small, but the "money taken in would support a score of country

[1] "Among the Materializers," *Nation*, XXXVIII (January 3, 1884), 9–10.

missionaries." Seats were in such great demand at the séances, according to Godkin, that they had "to be engaged long in advance." The sitters at the materializations were usually limited to about two dozen per séance. The "special personal spirits" assigned to each communicant were usually "of an extremely affectionate not to say demonstrative disposition" and they generally assumed the attractive form of ephemeral young ladies or gentlemen. The lucky sitter was allowed to "feel" the "embraces" of the supernatural visitor and "every effort was made to make him have a good time and come again."

Most of the sitters in these sessions were Americans of middle class, with a sprinkling of "speculative Germans, but very few Irish." The seating arrangements provided for an alternate placement of men and women. "The music, the dim light, and occasional excitement all inspired ease" and familiarity among the participants. The general tone was one of "earnest credulity, with a deceptive flavor of judicial inquiry, and light hearted chaff . . . thus new revelations were accepted on very easy terms." A typical visit to the sitting room of a Boston materialization séance may be illustrated by a report sent by the *Nation's* correspondent to editor E. L. Godkin:

But let us go to one of the seances and see the details. It is in the part of the city given over to cheap boarding-houses. The room is an ordinary one of some twelve or fifteen feet square, with a double row of chairs round three sides of it, and on the other the usual dark cabinet. In some cases, an alcove, or a small room curtained off from the one where the circle is held, takes the place of a cabinet. After the audience has assembled, the gas is extinguished, leaving only one lamp, which is screened by a curtain, so that there is barely light to show one's features to those who are close at hand, but not enough to show anything but the form a few feet off. Against the dark cabinet curtains figures clothed in black can hardly be distinguished, but the white forms are very clear. We look around and count twenty-three persons, including one or two men who sit or stand by the cabinet, partly to act as ushers or masters of ceremonies to the spirits, and partly to guard against awkward accidents. One of them has a music box with which he fills the pauses in the singing. We are told to keep our feet on the floor and not to cross our legs; but there is seldom any pretense of holding hands in the old way; and we dispose of ourselves in as easy a posture as the hard chairs will allow, and join in the singing. "In the sweet by and by," "There are angels hovering around," and "Beulah-land" seem the favorites, but we have occasionally more commanding ones, "Nearer my God to Thee," or lighter ones, like "Auld lang syne." From an artistic point of view they cannot be called entirely successful, but they keep us amused in the pauses, and for some curious psychological reason, most people feel more like singing in the dark, in a crowd, and are put at their ease by it.

We do not have to wait long. In a few instants there is a mysterious gleam of something white before the dark curtain behind which the medium has gone in her trance; the music pauses, and the more susceptible lean forward and draw long intense breaths. The white gleam becomes a veiled woman who advances into the room; and I feel my next neighbor tremble, and see the big drops of sweat start out on his forehead, and the woman on the other side leans heavily against my shoulder. The spirit beckons to some one; and a series of inquiries by the various members of the audience, "Is it me?" "Is it me?" presently shows that a young man is wanted who goes forward nearly to the curtain and is whispered to, embraced, and very audibly kissed; and the spirit then goes back behind the curtain, but re-appears again for a moment to exchange some more kisses. Then a similar performance is gone through by another spirit with another sitter, a young woman this time, who is so excited that she nearly faints away, the kissing being very animated and prolonged again—then and indeed all through the evening. The next phantom seems that of a little child, a mere baby, but it does not entirely emerge from the curtains. Then appears a female form in white tulle, which seems the favorite spiritual traveling costume even in wintry weather, and this one has a phosphorescent gleam in her hair and belt like imprisoned fire-flies, which is really very pretty in the dusky light. Another very neat little performance is that of materializing flowers. The spirit takes your hand and makes a series of little pats and passes, and presently you find a flower between your fingers, which you are told is fresh from spirit land. The rose I receive must have been a good while on the way, from its faded condition; but the mysterious effect was very well arranged.

Then comes a short delay, and a figure in man's clothes emerges from the cabinet and seats himself affectionately in the lap of a young woman and kisses her warmly. And we learn that he was a friend of her father's who has regained his youth in the other life to a degree very comforting to some of the members of our party. The young woman never knew him in the flesh (recognition seems very difficult in a large proportion of manifestations), but that counts for nothing in the happy abandon of spiritualism. Then come other forms, including a boy who dances round and balances a chair on his chin; and a very devotional nun. Presently a white-veiled woman summons one of the members of our party, whom she kisses and calls her darling, in longing whispers, somewhat to his embarrassment, as he is not aware of having before had the pleasure of her acquaintance—a brunette he afterwards describes her, with a firm, warm clasp of the hand, full clinging lips, and sleepy eyes. She wears very, very little clothing except her veil, and seems not only very human, but strikingly like a young woman whom he has since seen in the flesh. Presently she retreats to the curtain and "dematerializes" directly in front of it. This is one of the cleverest feats, as the form appears to grow gracefully shorter and fainter until it becomes a mere glimmer and melts away, leaving nothing but a rapidly disappearing white puddle of muslin against the opening in the curtains; and it adds very much to the effect of the scene.[2]

In Newark, New Jersey during the late 'sixties spiritualists began to attract new attention by opening a singular Sabbath School in the old Tenth Ward Fire Engine House on Bank Street. "This city," wrote an editor at that time, "has been blessed for the last five years with more than her due of spiritualists who while pretending holiness practice free love and deviltry, and corrupt the morals of all who come within their circle of influence." And, he added, the Sabbath School published books and pamphlets which combined "religion and lust" as a means of proselyting for their new faith. An example of the society's methods of attracting converts was a spectacular celebration staged on New Year's night of 1868, the twentieth anniversary of the beginning of spiritualism in Hydesville, New York.

At about nine o'clock on the eve of that New Year's day

street pedestrians were astonished to see the cult leader, James McEwen, standing in front of the open window clad in the habiliments of Adam before the fall, while the fair unclad form of 19 year old Miss Alithea Reeves,

---

[2] *Ibid.,* and for other material in a similar vein see Henry James, "Modern Diabolism," *Atlantic Monthly,* XXXII (August, 1873), 219–224; F. Perrone, "Spiritism and Modern Devilworship," *Dublin Review,* LXI (October, 1867), 253–280; "Demonology at Home and Abroad," *Blackwood's Magazine,* XCIX (April, 1866), 502–518.

impersonating Eve, was seen to flit to and fro under the gas-light, like a faun gamboling in the garden of Eden.

The "considerable gathering" of citizens collected around the converted fire engine house were told by sympathetic spiritualists mingling in the crowd that this "spectacle was gotten up on purpose to be seen as a revelation." The crowd before the large window was then invited into the temple by the "High-priest McEwen" who welcomed his visitors from his perch in the center of the large room standing like a "Roman orator without his toga expounding to the gathering the mysteries of the new creed."

As far as the members of the press, who rushed to the scene, could transcribe in these uncommon circumstances, the High Priest McEwen said that members of his cult, having reached a higher plane in human existence, were

entirely irresponsible for what they might do and utterly without sin; that they were in the same condition as Adam and Eve before the fall, and wholly cleansed from the lust of the world, the flesh and the Devil. They ignored human institutions, laws and customs and acted solely from the prompting of the Spirits which made men perfect.

As McEwen made his exposition, Miss Reeves remained standing in the costume of Eve and did not appear at all abashed at the scrutiny of the crowd of unbelievers.[3]

The police let the matter pass as part of the New Year's scene in Newark, but a few nights later, when the same revelation ceremony was repeated, Newark Police Chief William Clark raided the Temple and took the worshipers into custody. Eventually, the principals were brought to trial in the Essex County, New Jersey Court on January 28, 1868 before Judge J. C. Mills. The prosecution merely stated the facts of the case, but the defense pleaded that members of the cult believed that by abandoning their clothes and returning to the state of Adam and Eve they could banish the evil spirits which obviously dominated the world. Alithea Reeves testified that being seen in the nude

[3] New York *Times,* January 5, 1868.

was neither a sin nor even an indiscretion since "to the pure all things are pure." Judge Mills took exception to this point of view and committed all the principal members of the cult to the state insane asylum at Trenton.[4]

While the spirits may have been agents of devils or saints they were often a threat to the smooth working of the human institution of matrimony. This was especially true when widowers or widows attempted to re-engage themselves into these bonds. When these "lonely hearts" sought a new mate the spirits often intervened by "administering discipline." For example, in 1873, a Mr. Burchard of Missouri, having been a widower, had married again. After about three weeks his discipline began. Mysterious rocks began to drop on the roof in an unforeseen way during Mr. Burchard's absence and "on going out into the yard the family could see no person about, but to their consternation they saw rocks gradually rise from the ground and after ascending a sufficient height, drop down on the roof." Then, pillows and comforters behaved in a way to show displeasure with the present occupants of the marriage bed. One night the covers of the bed were rolled back by an unseen hand and in the handwriting of Mr. Burchard's first wife the following words were revealed: "These things shall continue forever!"

A Mr. Courtney of Oshkosh, Wisconsin had no more than merely contemplated a second marriage when weird lights began to appear in various parts of his house. To investigate this strange occurrence he called in a committee made up of members of the faculty of the local teachers' college. The pedagogues saw the strange light, a description of which they found horrible to relate. Its fire did not reflect but was "simply a flame with clearly defined edges, while all around was inky darkness." The committee poked around at the fire with various implements but was unable to determine its cause.[5]

In 1873, Mrs. John Sherman, a lonely widow in Buffalo, New York, who insisted that she had not even thought of remarriage was annoyed by a "shadowy *vehengericht.*" Her deceased husband's spirit would tramp invisibly into her bedroom and then "sitting down on the bed

---

[4] New York *Times,* February 4, 1868.
[5] New York *Times,* January 12, 1873.

would pull off his boots" and drop them on the floor. Friends hid in the clothes closet while the good widow ostensibly retired and they, too, clearly heard the boots drop. Some persons expressed the belief that perhaps the widow had not exactly told the truth when she asserted that she had never contemplated remarriage.

A widower in Louisville, Kentucky, in 1874, was similarly chastised by the spirits. Some time before his wife died she extracted from him the promise that no other woman should ever take her place and "this done she peacefully passed away." At first, the husband displayed a "proper amount of grief and black crape, but in a very brief time he began to take notice of another woman" and arranged to take her for his wife. But retribution was close at hand.

On the day of the ceremony the wedding cake was carefully locked in a vacant room to preserve it from the depredations of small boys in the neighborhood. The wedding ended, the happy pair went in search of the cake to distribute it to their friends . . . they found the cake utterly destroyed and its crumbs strewn on the floor.

Since the room was locked, members of the local press who were present concluded that the cake had been destroyed by the angry spirit of the man's dead spouse. The faithless husband was so shaken that he spent his second honeymoon under the care of special nurses in a Louisville hospital. These angels of mercy had been carefully instructed to guard the safety of their patient from the spirit of his "outraged" first wife—real or imagined.[6]

Sometimes the spirits seemed determined to break up a happy home of long standing. Colonel J. H. Blood, gallant officer of the Sixth Missouri Infantry Regiment, Treasurer of the City of St. Louis, and president of the St. Louis Railway Company, deserted his legal wife and fled the country with a "siren" named Helen Holland, because spirits had told him that this beauty was his true soul-mate.[7]

A most curious intrusion of the spirits into the institution of matrimony occurred in 1879 when Katie Eaton, daughter of Colonel Isaac E.

[6] *Ibid.*, June 19, 1874.
[7] New York *Times*, July 4, 1866.

Eaton of Leavenworth, Kansas married Benjamin Pierce, the son of a former president of the United States. This union was of particular curiosity because both the bride and the groom had been dead for many years. In fact, young Pierce was killed in an accident on the Boston and Maine Railroad on January 6, 1853 shortly before his father's inauguration and Katie had died years before that time at the age of three weeks.

Colonel Eaton, his wife, and his friend, Governor Wilson Shannon of Kansas, having been spiritualists for many years, had been in contact with the spirit of Katie Eaton for a period of several years. During one of these conversations Katie, who was then approaching spirit spinsterhood, delightedly informed her parents that she was engaged to be married to Benjamin Pierce, the son of President Franklin Pierce. The bridegroom, by that time a mature spirit-gentleman, had been a resident of "the Great Beyond" for twenty-five years. Thus, both the prospective bride and groom were adult spirits fully aware of whatever responsibilities matrimony might entail on the other side. Katie "communicated" to her parents all details telling them when the ceremony was to be performed and what arrangements had been made to transport the nuptial pair from the spirit-world to Colonel Eaton's residence in Leavenworth in order to attend a wedding supper.

This extraordinary feast was reported in the society pages of the Kansas press:

Accordingly, before the appointed time all the necessary arrangements had been perfected. A cabinet, for the accommodation of the famous medium, Dr. J. V. Mansfield, was prepared. Professor T. V. Mott and his wife came over from Memphis, Dr. Dooley came up from Kansas City, and everything was made ready for the interesting occasion. On the wedding evening there assembled at the residence of Colonel Eaton a select company consisting of the distinguished medium, the immediate family, Colonel H. D. Mackay, the president of the Alliance Life Insurance Company, and other illustrious persons of Kansas. The wedding feast was prepared, and the guests were on hand at the appointed hour. The room was partially darkened, and Professor Mott took his place to assist at the cabinet. Owing to the unusual force required to materialize two forms at the same time, Dr. Dooley also took a seat along with the professor. The table was spread, the guests were seated, places were reserved for the bride and groom, plates were laid for them, and an elegant bouquet placed at each place, according to the bride's directions. All was now ready for the appearance of those in whose honor the company had assembled, and the guests waited the appearance of the bridal party. But they had not long to wait. The announcement was soon made from the cabinet that the spirits were ready. The guests, one after another, were invited up to the aperture, where the lady and her husband were presented, both appearing with perfect distinctness and very lifelike, receiving the guests pleasantly, and entering freely into conversation with them. After this, both spirits walked out of the cabinet across the room, and took the places prepared for them at the table. The bride wore an elegant heavy satin dress, white as light, with the conventional flowing marriage veil and orange blossoms. The groom wore the regulation black broadcloth and white vest with full blown rose in the button-hole of the coat—though roses in this vicinity are now done blooming. This would seem to prove that in the Summer Land the roses bloom perpetually. After receiving the congratulations of their friends, and narrating the particulars of their marriage—explaining how and where in the spirit world the ceremony had been performed—the bridal party put off the semblance of mortal body and earthly habiliments, which they had donned for the occasion, and returned to their home in the spirit world, or, perchance, to their celestial wedding tour.

A day after the wedding, word came from the spirit world to the social editor of the Leavenworth *Times* giving a list of the names of over one hundred guests who had attended the spectral wedding in "the Summer Land." The list included members of the Eaton and Pierce families who were now residing in the spirit world as well as other leading American statesmen now deceased who took the occasion to attend the wedding of the son of a former president.[8]

While the union of Katie and Benjamin Pierce may have been made in heaven, the marriage of a seafaring gentleman, Captain John Freeman of San Francisco, was arranged by the spirits somewhat this side of "the Great Beyond." The sea captain, a shipmaster who usually sailed out of San Francisco, became interested in spiritualism and soon he began to hear words of ancient wisdom from tables, stools, and

[8] Leavenworth *Times,* June 25, 1879; for additional stories on this spirit wedding see the same paper on June 26, 1879 and the New York *Times,* June 29, 30, 1879.

other seafarers' furniture. He became convinced that his guardian spirit was that of an old pirate captain formerly of the Spanish main under whose instructions Captain Freeman often navigated his ship, sometimes with limited success. These difficulties prompted the captain to seek the aid of a lady medium.

This gentle person not only spoke well of the offending spirit of the old pirate but also explained to the bachelor Captain Freeman that he was soon to marry and that "his future bride would shortly be guilty of the indiscretion of exhibiting herself in the nude at the foot of his bed." The details of this interesting and impending episode, which were revealed in 1872 at the fascinating court trial of *Freeman* v. *Freeman,* indicated that the

worthy mariner laid awake in his bed on the following night in order to be in readiness for the expected enrapturing vision, and presently, as is the frequent habit of the mariner, he fortified himself for the encounter by means of one of those fluids known comprehensively as rum. At any rate the captain soon saw or fancied he saw the blessed damsel

sitting on the end of his bed. But he soon discovered that the nude lady who "leaned over the foot-board of his bed was not precisely out of Heaven," but rather was none other than the medium herself.

Being a believer in the admonitions of the spirits, the captain married the medium. In time, he found that he had also acquired a responsibility for the support of the medium's many relatives. The good mariner, not wishing to be a slave harnessed to support so large a family of spiritualists who seemed unfamiliar with the rugged requirements of earning a living in the real world, sued for divorce, and in the case of Freeman v. Freeman it was determined that if "a marriage contract was consummated with a female medium on the express admonition of the spirits the male party to the compact was at liberty at any time to claim undue duress and obtain an annulment." [9]

In the state of Iowa the spirits carried on their usual nefarious tricks of upsetting peaceful marital situations and the like, but in addition to this, unseen demons caused consternation in the fledgling textile industry which in 1874 was beginning to thrive in Des Moines. During

[9] New York *Times,* March 13, 1872.

the nocturnal hours, when the second floor shops along Cherry Street were dark, sewing machines ran furiously by means of "ghost power," thread was wasted, bobbins clogged, green and blue lights flashed, and bells were rung by demons having their own way in the shops. A private house on Locust Street was afflicted with green lights which moved around on a bedroom wall, while dogs along the street barked and snapped furiously at spirits in the air at night, and "phantom book-peddlers pulled bell cords." In a loose sort of way, prominent "intellectual" ladies of East Des Moines often visited with the "spectres" on Cherry Street. Sometimes the spirits followed these socialite friends to their homes and indiscriminately played their Swiss music boxes until unseemly hours of the night.[10]

Even gaolers in some parts of the United States were plagued by demons from the spirit world. In the summer of 1872 a prisoner named John Avery, having been condemned to death, was confined in the county jail of Hackensack, New Jersey. Eventually, in accordance with due process of law, Avery was dispatched to the world beyond. Three years later, a prisoner named Henry Wallace swore before the prison board that he had seen Avery's spirit walk around one of the tiers and pull the bedclothes off a German prisoner confined in a cell formerly occupied by Avery. The German confirmed the story and many prisoners who knew Avery now remembered that he had made a solemn promise to return to the Hackensack jail after his death. As was customary among the spectres, Avery's spirit returned just as the clock struck twelve—"a soft unusual light filled the whole interior of the jail and awakened all the prisoners. Some were terror-stricken and buried their heads beneath the bedclothing, while others seemed paralyzed and could not move." Prisoners solemnly averred that they heard windows raised, felt cold air rush in, and saw the shadowy form of a legless man gliding in between the bars and up the tiers of cells. The figure entered the cell formerly occupied by Avery, browsed around a bit and then disappeared the way he had entered.[11]

As was to be expected spirits often traveled upon public conveyances in American cities during the after-midnight hours. It was the generally

[10] Des Moines *Register,* quoted in New York *Times,* May 7, 1874.
[11] New York *Times,* March 11, 1875.

accepted belief that these beings preferred the night air rather than the brighter atmosphere of noonday. This preference was demonstrated in 1873 by an itinerant spirit which persistently appeared as a passenger upon the horse-drawn streetcars of Detroit. This spectre, said a contemporary observer, "appears in the form of a closely-veiled lady, clad in winter garments, which glides into a seat while the horses are in a trot, and rides until a fare is demanded, when it vanishes before the outstretched hand of the conductor, and is seen no more for the night." Several drivers encountered the mystical lady and all conductors agreed that when they approached her for a fare they "uniformly felt a creeping sensation up the spine and over the scalp." Cynics said the streetcar men created these tales merely to increase traffic and excitement on the owl car runs and many night revelers did begin to ride the cars in Detroit for the rollicksome purpose of taking liberties with strange young ladies upon the pretext of their wish to make a liaison with the spirit world.[12]

During the latter decades of the nineteenth century while many Americans living in the interior were encountering spectres and embracing spiritualistic sects, New York, the first spawning ground of the movement, continued to produce bizarre variations of spiritualism. On one warm afternoon in August the Spiritualist Baptist Church and Progressive Association held a baptism picnic on the East River, near Glen Cove to celebrate the baptizing of Professor Noyes Wheeler by Mrs. Marie Draper, the "Daughter of Zion," into the "Kingdom of the Bride."

As the party of pilgrims, including a choir of "young and beautiful girls," boarded the barge *William H. Norton* at the foot of Broome Street several young rowdies lounging around the Bowery door fronts leaped on board determined to go along and witness the sacred immersion and as the barge paused at other wharfs along the way more young Bowery residents came on board bringing with them their "ladies" who were "not of the spiritualistic faith but who were apparently not unused to spirits."

Professor Noyes Wheeler, about to be immersed into a sacred hier-

[12] *Ibid.,* August 29, 1873.

archy, was a man of about sixty years of age. His head was "covered with long whitish yellow hair," and his "long, gaunt, discolored face was ornamented by a straggling growth of faded yellow beard." The Daughter of Zion, according to an observer, was a "corpulent, double-chinned, middle-aged woman who weighs about three hundred pounds and is capable of a wonderful flow of ungrammatical language," a most extraordinary medium—"a favorite confidante of the Virgin Mary and more in the habit of associating with angels than mortals."

As the bargeload of pilgrims halted at the Morton Street landing for more of the faithful, additional citizens of the Bowery began to leap aboard, causing the captain of the tug moving the barge to demand a larger fee.

The professor, by this time ready to abandon the baptism ceremony planned for him later at Willett's Point, gazed down from the side of the barge and declared that water from the East River was too "filthy to be consecrated even by Divine Power." Then, according to newspaper accounts, the following colloquy took place between the professor and the Bowery boys who felt that they were being deprived of seeing a spectacle which had been promised:

First Boy,   "Look here, Professor, we must have the baptism somehow. Suppose we have it at the end of the pier?"

Professor,   "What—in this filthy water?"

Second Boy,   "So much the more need for purification."

Professor,   "It can't be, boys. The East River is too filthy to be purified. I have no control over the matter at all. I am controlled by the Daughter of Zion and she by the revolution of the spirit."

First Boy,   "Well, we must see you in your white robe anyhow. Put that on for us, and that will do."

Professor,   "It can't be done. The robe is in the Daughter's possession, and she made it at the direction of the angels. You don't understand, boys. She is the greatest medium in the world—lives in trances, sees spirits. Every day she goes among the angels in Heaven and sits at the feet of Virgin Mary, and at night she is with the angel Gabriel and the Lamb of God. If she has a revelation today, she will baptize me, otherwise she won't. There is no use trying to coax her; you won't have any effect on her if she does not receive a revelation from God."

The Bowery boys went to the Daughter of Zion and argued with her. She was kindly, but adamant, declaring that there could be no baptism unless she got the word. The Daughter was most critical of ordinary Baptists who baptize without a revelation. "They ain't no religion at all," she said, but "Spiritual Baptists is." Finding that there was no persuading the professor or the Daughter, the Bowery boys proposed that the whole party should proceed to Staten Island by ferry-boat, where the baptism could take place. The professor agreed to this plan if the consent of the Daughter could be obtained. When the Daughter was approached she hesitated, talked a great deal about "a revelation" but at length gave her consent and the "party proceeded merrily in anticipation of the spectacle." The barge was turned around and headed for the Whitehall Street ferry landing.

As the multitude romped off the barge and onto the ferry "three harpers" joined the gathering and soon the baptism party on board was alive with dancing while at the same time the professor attempted to explain the fine points of his faith amid the din and clamor.

When the party arrived at the Staten Island landing the professor, climbing on top of a railing and raising his two arms, arrested the debarking multitude long enough to dedicate his party as well as the miscellaneous throng of people awaiting the boat by singing his baptismal hymn augmented by the Girls' Choir of the Daughter of Zion in order to set the stage for the immersion:

> There on a broad, unruffled stream,
> The waters rolling by,
> She under the water plunges him—
> He cries "my friends, come nigh!"

At this point an incident occurred in singular contrast to the amusing one prevailing at that moment. One of Greeley's journalists who witnessed this scene was profoundly moved by what he saw:

While the merriment around the professor was at its height, [he wrote] Mrs. Draper, the Daughter, suddenly sprang to her feet, with closed eyes, her form perfectly rigid, and with a strangely solemn aspect, which instantly

attracted all eyes caused a hush to fall upon the crowd. She commenced
to speak in Spanish. There was probably no one there—no mortal one at
least—who understood the tongue; but the soft, musical diction fell from her
lips with a readiness and unconsciousness that instinctively convinced the
listener that it was pure Castilian. Not only the manner, but the entire
aspect of the woman was changed. Her unwieldy homely form was apparently lost in the grace and luster of a wonderful inspiration, and as she
swayed to and fro, and placed her hands upon her breast, the sweet, melo-
dious language gushed from her lips in a wild and pleading strain, as if it
were the passionate supplication and entreaty of some lost soul in misery
and pain more utter and profound than that which mortals know. It lasted
only about five minutes. Then her eyes were closed again; she opened them,
and sat down and was the same ordinary person she had been before.
But while the strange metamorphosis lasted, there was perfect and reverent
silence preserved throughout the large and flippant crowd, and it was some
moments after its conclusion before the merriment was recommenced.

When the Daughter had finished, the throng on board the ferryboat
proceeded on the way to Willett's Point. Many of the passengers who
were not members of the baptismal party or of the Bowery excursionists were "considerably bewildered as well as amused, by the rambling
dissertation" on spiritualism given to the crowd on the boat by the
professor. After a few moments a "Milesian female possessed of a considerable flow of language" became incensed by the professor's "unorthodox harangue" and "threw herself upon him" in a "vituperative
torrent of scriptural quotations" to prove that there was but one Church
"the Roman Catholic Church, out of the pale of which salvation was
an utter impossibility." After a "stormy discussion," the bewildered
professor was glad to retreat by fitfully agreeing to everything to which
the female Celt gave utterance and praising her for her "devotion to
the only true faith under the sun."

Four well known members of the New York sporting fraternity,
George Barnett, Frank Slater, Louis Reed, and Harry Jessup were most
interested spectators of the bout between the professor and the Milesian
woman. While the debate had been in progress these wagering gentlemen had taken bets as to the outcome and as the professor climbed

down from the podium after capitulating to orthodoxy, the four sporting gentlemen duly paid off their bets.

As the sporting men finished paying off, the party disembarked at Vanderbilt's Landing and paraded along the shore of the bay until they reached Willett's Point, the site chosen for the consecration. There upon the grassy banks, the old ladies of the party brought out their baskets of food and fed the hungry outsiders as far as their provisions went. At the same time the Daughter of Zion retired to a nearby cottage to put on her "Robe of Glory."

Everyone was impatient for the spectacle to begin except the professor. The representatives of the evening newspapers were particularly anxious for the baptism to begin so as to meet their evening editions. The professor "petulantly declared that he would be baptized when he pleased and that he would not be hurried for all evening papers in existence."

One of the sports who had laid wagers on the old gentleman's performance pressed a whiskey flask upon the professor urging him to partake of the stimulant as a fortification against a possible chill. "Wheeler smacked his lips, and took another, as if he liked it" adding that his indulgence was solely for the sake of medicinal considerations.

Shortly after the professor had finished taking his medicinal draught, an exclamation from part of the throng caused all eyes to turn in the direction of the nearby cottage. The Daughter of Zion appeared in her "Robe of Glory." Her ponderous figure was arrayed in a dress of white muslin. Upon her head was a huge sunbonnet, also of stiff muslin, and "her feet were encased in sandals bound upon her feet with blue ribbons."

As the Daughter approached the water's edge the professor immediately took off his outer conventional garments and appeared also in a white suit not unlike a set of "shirt and drawers" which gave his "skeletonic, ungainly form" an aspect which drew "some merriment" from the spectators. While the two moved across the beach sand to the water the professor "carried his walking stick which gave him the appearance of a nomadic dervish en route over the sand-hills to Mecca's shrine."

When the Daughter's blue-ribboned sandals touched the water a hundred of the faithful followers burst into the triumphal "Baptismal Hymn":

> In ordered ranks they slowly move,
> They are to the water bound,
> Two solemn faces full of love,
> Adoring while they sing.
>
> There on a broad unruffled stream,
> The waters rolling by,
> She under water plunges him—
> He cries, "my friends, come nigh!"

As the two broke into the waves, many of the sports and the Bowery crowd called out triumphantly, "Go in, professor! You're on the road to glory."

The Daughter grasped the professor by the waist and "dexterously plunged him out of sight" several times, "bringing him up dripping like a bunch of drabbled seaweed."

When the ceremony had been completed the two principals returned to the beach where everyone congratulated the professor on the glory he had attained. A sophisticated journalist who had watched the spectacle as one interested in human behavior and had remained on the periphery of the large throng which massed around the dripping professor, remarked that although the old gentleman was undoubtedly "cracked," he was "certainly a gallant old fellow." As the excursionists returned to Manhattan all agreed that they had "enjoyed a rare spectacle." [13]

Four days later, Margaret Fox's friend Horace Greeley, who was the recipient of an avalanche of letters concerning the "religious extravagance" which had taken place at Willett's Point, printed an editorial on the subject. In his view the exhibition of the "Daughter of Zion," was but one more example of the legion of strange spiritualistic faiths which marked the decades of the mid-nineteenth century. "In modern times," said Greeley, "we have had Jumpers, Sandemanians, Muggletonians and Mormons, Dunkers and Mysties." There was no "folly great

---

[13] New York *Tribune,* August 12, 1865; for a similar story see New York *Times,* August 12, 1865.

enough," he wrote, "to repel all mankind." Whoever pleased and took enough trouble could set up a religion.

The great safety, he said, against errors of the people was to be found in the

toleration which in this country, at least, has become one of our social and intellectual habits. If the old gentleman, who the other day was baptized into the "Kingdom of the Bride" should be arrested, and taken to the Tombs, and racked, and put upon a bread and water diet and finally hung for his heresy in the East River, twenty other gentlemen would at once rush to the rescue and demand to be baptized by Mrs. Draper, the "Daughter," and be seriously disappointed if, in their turn, they were not racked and hung. Under such management "The Kingdom of the Bride" would not fail to wax until, the hangings and burnings all over, it would have a splendid church on Fifth Avenue, with Mrs. Draper regularly settled over it, at a salary of $10,000 per annum, with a genteel parsonage thrown in rent free.

Fortunately, said Greeley, the authorities have the wisdom to restrain the cries of the intolerant who would curb excesses which arise in the name of religion.[14]

Spiritualism's progress at this time was marked by large annual conventions held in various parts of the nation. A typical gathering was one held in Pratt's Hall on Broad Street, in Providence, Rhode Island in 1867. This city was chosen "on account of its peculiar fame" as a haven for "heretics—the refuge of Roger Williams, the home of religious toleration."

A foreign traveller who visited this gathering was "struck with the wild and intellectual appearance" of the delegates whose eyes were "preternaturally bright" and "faces preternaturally pale." "Nearly all the men wore long hair and nearly all the women were closely cropped." The meeting place was filled with both "mortals and angels" and in Broad Street as well as in the hall, "angels stood in the doorways, spectres flitted about the room. Their presence was admitted, their sympathy assumed, and their counsel sought. A dozen times the speakers addressed their words, not only to the delegates present in the flesh, but to heavenly messengers who had come to them in the spirit."

[14] New York *Tribune,* August 16, 1865.

L. K. Joslin, a local spiritualist leader, welcomed the delegates to the Rhode Island city of refuge. "Today," he said to the listening throng, "the Spiritualists of the United States are the Great Heretics, and as such the Spiritualists of Providence greet you with their welcome believing that you are infidel to the old heresies that cursed rather than blessed our whole humanity. . . ." The speaker proclaimed that this gathering was not "alone," for there were others at the doors.

Those of other ages, fearless, true and martyred in the earth-life for their devotion to the truth—the cherished, wise and good of the long-ago, and the loved ones of the near past—they will manifest their interest in, and favour with their presence the largest body of individuals on this continent who realize their actualized presence and power. And unto them, as unto you, we give the meeting.

Loud cheers and applause from the audience indicated a general welcoming of the unseen delegates from the world beyond.

As the deliberations progressed, Warren Chace, a spiritualist leader from Illinois, declared from the platform that millions of Americans had become believers in spiritualism. "Not even the Methodists," he said, could equal them in numbers and "the spiritualists count in their ranks some eminent men, shrewd lawyers, gallant soldiers, graceful writers," and, it was true, a few persons who could "hardly escape the suspicion of being simple rogues and cheats." A society of millions of persons, he reminded them, had political, as well as spiritual power.

Mr. Chace and other speakers declared that the old religious gospels were exhausted, that the churches founded by them were dying on the vine, that new revelations were now required by men. The great events, signs, and phenomena which had occurred since Margaret and Katherine Fox first heard the new word in Hydesville offered "an acceptable ground-plan for a new, a true, and a final faith in things unseen."

A tone of "stern hostility" toward moral creeds and standards of all Christian nations marked the speeches of the men and women of the convention. This was "not the age of worship," they said, "but of investigation." Mr. John Finny, in a ringing voice, cried out to the delegates that "The old religions are dying out. We are here to represent a new religion!"

John Pierpont, of Washington, D.C., an aged clergyman and once a scholar at Yale's famed divinity school exclaimed, "I am an infidel to a great many of the forms of popular religion because I do not believe in many of the points which are held by a majority of the Christians"; he put his faith, he said, not in "creeds and cannons," but in "progress, liberty, and spirits." [15]

Ten days after he had delivered this speech the old Reverend Pierpont died. A few days later, Mrs. John Conant, a well known Boston medium, announced "that she had got his soul back again in her drawing-room; a presence visible to her, sensible to some, audible to many." Charles Crowell and J. M. Peebles of Boston said that on one occasion Mrs. Conant fell into a spirit-trance as the soul-spirit of John Pierpont passed into her body and spoke to them through her lips of affairs in "the Great Beyond." After being "fixed" by occult powers, Mrs. Conant's facial expression froze into "an earnest and steady gaze" and then the voice of the Reverend Pierpont's spirit uttered this "immortal sentence" through the lips of the medium: "Brothers and sisters, the problem is now solved with me. And because I live, you shall live also." [16]

While some scholars and writers succumbed to the spectres of spiritualism, Mark Twain (or Samuel L. Clemens) was not one of these. In San Francisco he investigated "the new wildcat religion" at length during the 1860's and in an article appearing in the *Golden Era* he wryly complained that this "wretched delusion called spiritualism" had consumed more space in the San Francisco *Bulletin* than had the vital news of the day. Implying that the "city fathers" of San Francisco had become "subdued, subjugated by spiritualism," Mark Twain wrote that "the *Bulletin* and I will soon have to record the departure of the Board of Supervisors for Stockton. Poor creatures—to have kept out of the asylum on one pretext or another so long and then to fall at last through so weak a thing as spiritualism." [17]

Watching the continuing growth of spiritualism in the 1870's, the New York *Tribune* warned its readers to disregard

[15] William Hepworth Dixon, *New America*, II, 145–164.
[16] *Ibid.*, p. 165.
[17] Samuel L. Clemens [Mark Twain], *The Washoe Giant in San Francisco*, pp. 129–133, 133–134, and *passim*.

the popular idea that the spiritualist is very like the ancient abolitionist—ignorant, lantern-jawed, long-haired wild-eyed men and women in bloomers. Very few such people will be found among them. The Brahmin class of spiritualists embrace, both here and in Europe, men and women of high culture and unsettled religious faith, groping for truth in every new hypothesis set before them; among them were the Trollopes, Mrs. Browning, and many Bostonians well known as leaders in the literary and social world.

Below this brahmin class of leaders, said the *Tribune*, were the millions who made up the great mass of the spiritualists. These persons were downright obstinate people, of coarse minds, destitute of imagination or emotional faculties, whose hope or idea of a future life is not outraged by this revelation of stupid chair-lifting, table-thumping souls loafing through eternity, who can prescribe for a congested liver or give a useful hint as to railway shares.[18]

The New York *Times* expressed similar concern: "The operations of the public mediums are but straws on the surface of the vast ocean of popular interest which this assumed revelation has set in motion." And on November 19, 1874 Dr. George M. Beard delivered a lecture before a medical society in Brooklyn that had assembled the elite of the profession in the New York area to consider what measures ought to be taken against the danger arising from the cult. The contest of the century, Dr. Beard told the physicians, was not between Protestantism and Romanism but between civilization and barbarism as personified in the spiritualistic cult. The duty of scholars and scientists was to meet the wave of spiritualism and clairvoyance before the "delusion rolls over the country." This "superstition now has its bloody hands upon the throat of the Republic and will strangle it if it can." The new cult, he asserted, fed upon "the love of the living for the loved ones passed beyond." If you wanted to find "barbarism you need not cross mountains nor the seas, one-third of the population of this country is in a state of comparative degradation" where cults such as spiritualism had sunk their roots. Spiritualism, he said, is "as old as human ignorance." There was a direct link between the "witchcraft excitement in Salem and the rise of the spirit rappings in Rochester." The "majority of semi-savages every-

---

[18] New York *Tribune*, July 24, 1879.

where have always been spiritualists." The problem they had met to ponder, he concluded, was "a contest between reason and passion," between the fourteenth and the approaching twentieth century.[19]

The spiritualists met such "slanderous assaults" by retorting that "the clergy would never admit the truth nor the politicians, but the ugly fact was that the struggle between Christianity and spiritualism would soon come, the issue could never be resolved." The "inventions of the Christian clergy," they said, "had caused all the world's ills." Spiritualistic manifestations had done more, they grandly claimed, for "humanity in teaching a belief in immortality than all that Jesus Christ ever did." [20]

[19] New York *Times*, November 20, 1874.

[20] New York *Times*, August 11, 1879; for another story on the conflict between the Spiritualists and the orthodox clergy see the New York *Times*, October 11, 1885.

AS THE TWIG IS BENT THE TRE

The Haunted Halls of Learning

THE INFLUENCE OF Margaret Fox was felt in many areas of community life. While men of science, as well as committees at Harvard, Yale, and the University of Pennsylvania, were troubled by the spirits, more humble institutions were also annoyed by spectres in their midst. Perhaps the situation at the Charles Street School in Newburyport, Massachusetts, in 1873 may serve as typical of the hundreds of "haunted school houses" which presented a peculiar dilemma for pedagogues and school boards during the nineteenth century.

The Charles Street School was presided over by Miss Abigail Perkins, a teacher with a strong practical mind and an abhorrence of anything as "silly as spiritualism." But one day, according to the voluminous minutes of the School Committee of Newburyport which carried on an exhaustive investigation into the matter of the Spectral Ghost-boy at Charles Street School, Miss Perkins' pupils told her that "a strange boy was up to tricks at the window sometimes putting his head up to the glass and looking in." After receiving such information from the students several times Miss Perkins moved her desk so that she would have a constant view of the window.

A few days later the boy's figure appeared again on a stairway from which he could gaze into the school room through a window. With her ruler in her hand the teacher advanced toward the mysterious boy who stood waiting quietly. He possessed, she told the committee,

one of the prettiest faces she had ever seen, with a sweet smile on his beautiful lips, needing a kiss more than a blow. His body was dressed in neat white clothes, his hair was almost white; his face was as pale as death, and his eyes a sweet blue. His face was older than his years and he had the appearance of wisdom beyond his years. She advanced to him, and then he dodged to the attic stairs. She followed near enough to take hold of him, but he was not there. He seemed to sink through the stairs, and where she would grasp his person her hand struck the floor. He was gone.

This strange event at the school house sent the pupils home with lips buzzing. In a few days the School Committee was forced to close the grounds to the hundreds of adult visitors who stood for hours waiting for a glimpse of the spirit-boy. The metropolitan newspapers sent their representatives and the local police were urged to "show some results." A bad, truant-prone boy was arrested, charged and put away as a "disturber of the peace," but still the face of the spirit-boy now and then appeared at the window. Some townspeople said that the teacher was a witch and ought to be discharged. When crowds of adults continued to collect around the school to watch, a carpenter was sent to nail up the passageway to the attic, but even so, the spirit-boy could be heard knocking and sawing in the attic and now and then he reappeared to glance momentarily in at the teacher and the pupils.[1]

Henry J. Raymond of the *Times,* noting the fascinating dispatches relating to the spectral small boy in New England, dipped his pen in editorial ink and conjectured that perhaps the ghostly youngster had a just grievance. "That ancient school-house in Newburyport," he wrote, "where scores of youthful Yankees have struggled with the spelling book, and been grounded in grammar, by the aid of the teacher's angu-

---

[1] New York *Times,* January 11, 1873; for a few added details see copy of Minutes of the Newburyport School Board, 1873, ms.

lar and convincing ruler" may be justly haunted by the "supernatural small boy, who flattens his ghostly nose at available windows and thrusts his spectral head through vacant stove-pipe holes." The editor stated categorically that his newspaper supported the right of small boys' spirits to haunt a school house and found little sympathy for the selectmen of Newburyport who sought in vain to nail up his ports of entry.[2]

In a few weeks the Newburyport ghost-boy was a national figure. While every newspaper in the land was following the curious antics of the spectral-boy the citizens of Newburyport were sorely divided over the true cause of disturbance at their school. A committee of reputable citizens including an editor, the selectmen and a deacon investigated the affair. The selectmen and the deacon were anxious to disprove the theory of supernatural influence, but the editor, it seems, was reluctant to "spoil so fruitful a theme."

A majority on the committee wishing to intrude their explanation of the phenomena talked severely of hypothetical and ingeniously mischievous boys and of novel or ill-conducted winds as the actual spirits which interrupted the school. The teacher, standing firmly in the face of ridicule and interrogation, stoutly denied that "mortal boys and winter winds could produce the apparitions and the noises" which had disturbed her classes. She had "clutched the hair of the ghostly small boy, and simultaneously seen him vanish into the air"; could any intelligent person, she demanded of the interrogators, be convinced "by mere assertion that the ordinary small boy when seized by the hair, is capable of vanishing from sight, leaving not a lock behind him?" And furthermore, she had struck her "agile tormentor with her ruler, but the blow had met with no resistance." As to the "juvenile face, which, with its ghostly nose flattened against the window or its spectral hair waving from an inaccessible stove-pipe hole," the beleaguered Miss Perkins challenged the committee to prove that the face was one of her mortal scholars.

The interrogators, hoping to quiet the disturbance at the school by intimating that it was either the work of truants or a psychological de-

---

[2] New York *Times*, January 12, 1873.

lusion were frustrated when a majority of the citizens of Newburyport "strongly enlisted on the side of the school teacher, as a truthful person mysteriously troubled by a supernatural small boy."

Finally, on a Saturday early in May, 1873, several months after the ghost-boy had first pressed his nose against the windowpane, a committee from the town visited the school determined to reach a final decision. As they sat in the scholars' seats deliberating a dust pan was flung into the group from the attic by what appeared to be supernatural means. Angered by this affront to their constituted authority, the committee took drastic action. They agreed to discharge Miss Perkins at once and to abandon the school at the close of the term.[3]

During the late 'seventies many Americans noticed that an alarming number of persons in the teaching profession appeared to be sympathetic to spiritualism. And this fear was substantiated one morning in May of 1879 when the school board and general public of New York City learned that the respected Professor Henry Kiddle, long-time superintendent of the city's school system, secretly had been a believing spiritualist for years and that he had written a book, *Spiritual Communications,* which was at that moment being taken off the presses. William Wood, president of the board, immediately asked Mr. Kiddle to resign on the grounds that he was "no longer worthy to hold the post." Mr. Kiddle refused to oblige.[4]

For several months rumors had been circulating around City Hall pertaining to Kiddle's affinity with the spirits, but the issue did not become critical until the publication of the superintendent's startling book. Immediately, members of the school board were forced to take a public stand upon the issue of spiritualism. Board member Benjamin F. Manierre said that the superintendent was employing his high position to sell his book and his ideas. "He is," wrote this board member, "the head of the largest school system in the world, having supervision over about 3,000 teachers. If he had been less dignified his book would have been passed over with contempt, as it appears to be a collection of rubbish. . . . He had no right to use his position to give publicity to his

[3] New York *Times,* March 8, 1873.
[4] New York *Times,* March 8, 1873; for an additional follow-up story see the *Times* for March 10, 1879.

absurd notions." Another board member, a lawyer named Samuel G. Jelliffe, after giving Kiddle's book careful study came to the conclusion that the superintendent's mind had become impaired. Yet he did not want the superintendent removed without substantial charges. School Commissioner Julius Kaizenberg, also a trustee of Temple Emanuel, was critical and could not see "Mr. Kiddle in the role of a prophet." Ex-mayor Wickham said that he had the highest respect for Mr. Kiddle, but not for his "delusion." But in the ex-mayor's opinion, the superintendent had as much right to be a spiritualist as he, Wickham, had to be a Presbyterian.[5]

The city, already in an uproar over this insidious threat to its school children, then learned that the normal schools were infested with spiritualists and Dr. Edward R. Chapin of King's County Asylum testified that the new cult was the cause of overcrowding in his institution; in fact, "some instructors from City College were already in the asylum because of worry over spirits." A public meeting of the school board was called to deliberate over what action ought to be taken and a large

[5] New York *Times,* May 5, 1879.

crowd assembled to hear the proceedings. Some members recommended that Kiddle be summarily discharged at once, asserting that anyone who had read his book would have to agree that Kiddle was mentally ill. Since Mr. Kiddle refused to attend the meeting, the majority of the board voted to table the matter temporarily to allow time for calm reflection. This courtesy, they felt, was due Mr. Kiddle because of his many years of devotion and service to the city's public schools.[6]

Although the superintendent refused to attend the meeting, he nevertheless held his ground and wrote long letters to the press asserting that he had been in actual contact with the spirits. Former "intellectual splendor and study" were nothing, he said, when compared with "recent spiritual progress. . . Harvey, Galileo, and Morse had also been ridiculed in their day." Mr. Kiddle did not propose to step aside voluntarily.[7]

At later hearings other school officials were called in to testify. Benjamin D. L. Southerland, principal of Grammar School Number Three and president of the New York Teachers Association, admitted that various rumors about the new book by Mr. Kiddle had been circulated among the teachers for several weeks. He added that while some of his colleagues were spiritualists most of the teachers felt that Mr. Kiddle had made a fool of himself. Lafayette Olney, principal of Grammar School Number Four said that he was utterly shocked because the superintendent, in his view, was the "last man we would have suspected of spiritualism," and how many more teachers of this faith there were in the system and where they were located Principal Olney said he would not venture to say.

Professor David B. Scott of the Normal College, whose wife was the daughter of the well known William Beldon, Jr., and who figured prominently in Kiddle's book, was most reluctant to commit himself on the subject of spiritualism. He denied that he had ever been present when Kiddle's daughter, Mrs. L. P. Weismann, communicated with the spirits, but he admitted that he had seen communications written to Mrs. Weismann from the spirit world by the famed Indian chieftain

[6] New York *Times,* May 8, 1879.
[7] New York *Times,* May 8, 1879.

Tecumseh "written in letters one to two inches long covering a large page with very few words."

It seems that several months previously Mrs. Weismann had suddenly become aware of the fact that she was a powerful medium. One day "she felt a peculiar sensation in her right arm, and her hand in which a pencil had been placed began to move by an external force." During the next few days she began to write messages not only from the spirits of dead relatives and friends but also from such great souls in the Summer Land as Lord Byron, William Shakespeare, William Cullen Bryant, and George Washington. She even received a message from Henry J. Raymond, the famed editor of the *Times* who had then but recently passed on. "I am tasting of joys I never knew on earth," wrote Raymond's spirit. "I was in error not to have believed in spirits [while on earth]. I suffered for it; but now I am purified."

At several teachers' meetings Mrs. Weismann was said to have contacted the spirit of Edgar Allan Poe who reported that the financier, James Fisk, Jr., was now a reptile in the world beyond; Boss Tweed, having at first been forced to take on the aspect of a reptile, due to his unusual political skill, had managed to better his position and now occupied a high station. With Poe's assistance James Fisk sent the following description of his unhappy place of torment to Kiddle's daughter: "Horror of horrors! I am surrounded by black darkness—so black I can almost feel it! Oh! To myself I seem as a log plunged into the water. So choked I feel, oh, I cannot swallow. I gasp! I drowned. Oh, I shall die! Help!"

Assistant Superintendent William Jones defended the name of Kiddle's daughter.

She has been [he said] an intimate of my family and is a young lady thoroughly womanly in every respect. Her whole heart has been devoted to music, and as a pianist she excels. She is amiable, honest, sincere—qualities which probably account for the implicit faith which her father places in the spirit communications coming in through her.

Jones thought it was an injustice to punish Mr. Kiddle and his daughter merely because she possessed these remarkable powers.

The school board was thus faced with a serious dilemma. Some of the members were for Kiddle's immediate dismissal, others felt that the pedagogue's forty years of service in the system ought to be respected as well as the feelings of the thousands of spiritualists in the city. Finally, Commissioner Wheeler addressed the crowd at the hearing: "This is a painful and embarrassing subject, and I have no desire to debate it . . . The strain on our teachers and scholars is too, too great" to leave the issue unresolved. Since it was a "matter of very great importance," a special committee would be set up to determine how far these beliefs had penetrated into the school system. He promised further action in a few days.[8]

Two weeks later the board called another meeting. It was announced that Mr. Kiddle had agreed to resign and in return the board passed a very flattering resolution praising the superintendent for his forty years of faithful service. In closing, the president said that all were pleased that this conclusion of the spirit matter had permitted all to "avoid a discussion of the vexatious question to which Mr. Kiddle's recent course had given rise." [9]

Leading spiritualists in the city immediately called Kiddle's dismissal "religious intolerance" and the "resolution cowardly avoidance of the facts." The superintendent, they said, had been forced out because of his religion. "How long," they cried, "shall this insolence be tolerated by a great people, that probably outnumbers any other religious community in the country?" Other religions, they said, "may make Milton's majestic devil the cornerstone of their religious faith; they may embrace legions of little devils whose function it is to torture souls of men, women, and little children forever" but they could not abide Kiddle's beliefs.[10]

The spiritualists mobilized to strike back at their malefactors. A corporation was formed with Henry Kiddle and Charles Partridge as leading officers and with many prominent citizens of New York City and Albany as stockholders. The expressed purpose of this corporate enterprise was to set up "practical communications" with the "other

[8] New York *Tribune*, May 8, 1879.
[9] *Ibid.*, May 22, 1879.
[10] *Ibid.*, May 21, 1879; also see "Minutes of the New York City School Board," 1879, ms.

side."[11] Kiddle continued his writing and lecturing for the cause. On January 4, 1880 he addressed a large mass meeting in Philadelphia during which he recited a poem entitled "Life" which he claimed had been composed by the spirit of William Shakespeare.

Philosophers [said Henry Kiddle in Philadelphia] have been seeking to solve the mystery of human life without success, for ages; one would suppose that at the very first intimation that light had dawned upon this mystery, all mankind would rush with throbbing hearts and eager footsteps to listen to the glad tidings, and to look behind the dark curtain which has hitherto hung between the visible and invisible worlds.

But this was not the case, said Kiddle. Although millions believed, the vast number of Americans, in their ignorance, saw spiritualism as a "kind of diabolism—an engine of Satan for ensnaring souls"; thus it was, said Kiddle, that many schoolmen and clergymen had refused to read his book. Spiritualism was now being persecuted as Christianity had been in the days of Tacitus. It was seen as "a pernicious superstition" and its advocates were classed as "fanatics and madmen," but the new faith would triumph, said Professor Kiddle. "Scientific bigots once contended against the Copernican system, the circulation of the blood, the rotation of the earth on its axis," but now all the nation's schools taught the truth of these principles. The day would soon come, predicted Kiddle, when the schools would also accept the basic principles of modern spiritualism.[12] Unfortunately, by the late decades of the nineteenth century, Mr. Kiddle's lofty hopes for further development of the faith founded by the Fox sisters failed to materialize.

[11] New York *Times,* July 11, 1881.
[12] *Ibid.,* January 5, 1880.

The Descent of the Medium into the Spirits' World

As FOR MARGARET Fox who had created this circus of spiritualism, the 1880's were lean years for her. The Civil War had marked a temporary decline in spiritualism, except in California, and at the close of the war Margaret had published her memoirs—the letters from Dr. Elisha Kent Kane. The book did not enjoy a wide sale since at that time there were other more exciting books on the post-war scene to compete with it. When spiritualism regained its popularity in the country as soon as the war was over, Margaret again returned to the tables. Despising the life of a medium she kept on with it only because it gave her a living in return for a few hours of work per week. Her "sorrows and her conscience" she began to solace with wine.

Margaret continued to fear her sister Leah who wanted her to join an organized cult. "I owe all my misfortune to that woman, my sister," said Margaret on one occasion, "and I have asked her time and time again: 'now that you are rich why don't you save your soul?' " [1]

In order to stay away from Leah, Margaret had spent years in the late 'seventies and early 'eighties travelling about the United States holding small séances in hotels and even in boarding houses. During these itinerant years she had kept her soul in some degree of quiet by lonely nights of drinking. Following these depressive nights she would tell astonished persons who came to ask for a sitting that she "loathed the thing . . . you are driving me into Hell." Yet a seeress must live. And Margaret stayed at the table, for it was the only work she seemed fitted to do. When she had some funds accumulated she said "I would drown my remorse in wine." But when she awakened once again she would "brood over" her life and the "miserable deception" it had been from the time when she was a little girl. Thus Margaret lived the life of an aging gypsy seeress moving from one dreary hotel to another.[2]

In the end, however, she always returned to New York City where she could hide or drink or hold her séances without arousing any ire. Indeed, it was in a small house on West 44th Street that she once again set up a lonely little place for herself, one that was somewhat more permanent than any she had known for many years.

In February of 1886 Commodore Joseph H. Tooker, a man who had always laughed at spirits, happened to attend a séance at Margaret Fox's little house on West 44th Street in New York, which he said was pretentiously furnished. He was ushered into a small reception room hung with curtains where several persons were waiting to interview relatives "who had gone before." When the Commodore's turn came he entered the medium's sitting room. She was

a middle-aged and very pale lady who had just risen from a bed of sickness. I made up my mind [he said] to ask no questions and so she did all the talking, which occupied fully three-quarters of an hour. In a moment she took my hands in hers and gracefully sank back into deep thought. She possessed a great magnetism, for the touch of her fingers produced a pricking sensation as if I were holding the hands of an electric battery.

[1] Davenport, *Death-Blow*, pp. 35–36; for similar details see New York *Herald*, September 21, 1888.
[2] Rochester *Union*, April 13, 1886.

The Commodore was greatly surprised at her familiarity with the names of his dead relatives and acquaintances which passed through his mind. Her descriptions of those he was thinking of were surprisingly accurate. It left him puzzled, for he found no way to account for such talent.[3]

Early in 1888, tiring of the weary séances and the fearsome criticism of her wealthy sister Leah, Margaret accepted substantial funds from her friend the wealthy London physician, Dr. H. Wadsworth of 21 Queen Anne Street, to take a trip to England in the interest of the cult. As she stepped off the steamer at an English port and was greeted by Wadsworth she told him, "I think too much of you to deceive you, there is nothing to spiritualism, it's a fraud." The doctor nodded, replying that he appreciated her frankness, "but he still seemed credulous" and wanted to proceed with the experiments.

Then, in the homes of wealthy English devotees of the New Jerusalem she began to take part in the most advanced aspects of the new worship, a kind of "materialization" which produced a physical picture of spirits behind a large "luminous paper" screen—the figure usually taking the exciting form of a young woman "virtually nude."

A few years later Margaret revealed some of the "dreadful" and "horrible hypocrisies" which she said were practiced in London by some extremists in the name of spiritualism.

They go even so far as to have what they call "spiritual children"! They pretend to something like the immaculate conception! . . . there are other seances, where none but the most tried and trusted are admitted, and where there are shameless goings on that vie with the secret Saturnalia of the Romans.[4]

In September of 1888 Margaret booked passage on board the steamer *Italy* and returned to New York. Her conscience and her distaste for the deceit of her mediumship multiplied by a depression growing out of her habit of seeking comfort in wine, turned her thoughts toward

[3] New York *Times,* February 14, 1886.

[4] New York *Herald*, September 25, 1888; for related information see A. Goodrich-Freer, *Essays in Psychical Research, passim;* New York *World*, October 21, 1888; Davenport, *Death-Blow,* pp. 50–51; Katherine H. Porter, *Through A Glass Darkly: Spiritualism in the Browning Circle, passim.*

some permanent surcease from unhappiness. Sometimes, she said, she contemplated "making a sweeping confession of the whole imposture." At other times her mood "in intervals of nervous excitement turned to the thought of suicide." Troubles weighed upon her while she was aboard the *Italy* in the vast Atlantic. "I do believe," she said, "that I should have gone overboard but for the Captain, and the doctor and some of the sailors." [5]

During the previous summer the notorious spiritualist Madam Diss De Barr, had been exposed in New York as a fraud. As Margaret came down the gangplank of the *Italy* upon reaching New York, reporters asked her for a comment upon the exposure of Madam De Barr. Margaret told the members of the press that she was revolted by the grossness of the De Barr fraud and added the assertion that "spirits never return." When the reporters expressed surprise upon hearing one of the mothers of the cult "deny the spirits," Margaret promised them that one day she would give "an interesting exposure of the fraud." Soon after Margaret reached her home a man from the *Herald* called as a follow-up on the promised story.

At the house on 44th Street the reporter was greeted by a small magnetic woman then about 54 years old, somewhat careless in her dress and marked by a certain frantic nervousness in her manner; her face bore "the traces of much sorrow and of world-wide experience." To the newsman's astonishment she seated him in a grand manner and after some simple queries appeared to be perfectly willing to tell him the weird story of her life.

"The world of humbug-loving mortals," she said, had verily trapped her as a young girl into the deceit which had been her life; now, she was willing to even the score "by making a clean breast of all her former miracles and wonders." As she flung out the long repressed story the medium paused now and then to sob and sometimes to leap to the piano "and pour forth fitful floods of wild, incoherent melody, which coincided strangely with that reminiscent weirdness which, despite its cynical reality, still characterized the scene."

Then in the midst of this dramatic revelation of fraud and humbug,

[5] New York *Herald,* September 24, 1888.

the medium paused. Suddenly the floor beneath the reporter's feet seemed to be alive with rapping. The startled man got up and walked about the room. The rappings followed him, seemed to cling to the furniture and then dart under tables clearly to harass the agent of the press. The clairvoyant, with shrieks of laughter, then seated herself by the piano and immediately a whole shattering of raps "resounded throughout its hollow structure."

Noting that the *Herald*'s man was by that time looking toward the door, Miss Fox, in a shrill and cynical observation, called out to the spirits to note how easily a gentleman of the press could be fooled.

She explained that for years after Kane's death she had been chained to a vast depression and to "brain fever" and that when she recovered she returned to the loathesome tables for a livelihood. "I have explored the unknown as far as human can," she said. "I have gone to the dead so that I might get from them some little token," but none came. She had even been in graveyards at night and had "sat alone on gravestones that the spirits of those who slept underneath might come to me. I have tried to obtain some sign. Not a thing! No, no, the dead shall not return." [6]

When the *Herald*'s story of the medium's confession reached the public it created a sensation. Those who had faith in spiritualism—and there were many—claimed that the poor woman was plainly drunk. Leah refused to comment, but her husband insinuated that both Margaret and Katherine would be in less trouble if they stayed sober.[7] At a public gathering of spiritualists in Adelphi Hall several mediums declared that Margaret had lost her senses because of excessive indulgence in drink.[8]

Margaret held herself in seclusion until the third week in October when she released a long story of her life exclusively to the New York *World*. On Sunday morning of October 21, 1888 the editors ran the life story of Margaret Fox on the first two pages of the *World*. An added feature was the announcement that on the same evening at the

[6] New York *Herald,* September 24, 1888.
[7] Davenport, *Death-Blow*, p. 43.
[8] New York *Herald,* September 25, 1888.

Academy of Music the great medium would deliver a lecture-demonstration exposing the "fraud of spiritualism." [9]

That night the Academy was filled to capacity. Some of the spectators came to witness a final end to humbuggery. But large numbers of others came to defend their faith in spiritualism. Dr. C. M. Richmond, a well known New York dentist, presided at the meeting and introduced Margaret Fox to the audience.

According to one garbled account, when Margaret rose to speak it was clear that she was much too nervous to confess orally what she had already permitted to be published in the New York *World*. Her friends, immediately perceiving her predicament, according to this eyewitness, set Margaret to the task of demonstrating how she had, for all the past years, produced her famous rappings.

"The entire house became breathlessly still . . . If her tongue had lost its power her preternatural toe joint had not." On the surface of a plain little wooden stool she "produced those mysterious sounds which for forty years frightened and bewildered hundreds of thousands of people in this country and Europe." [10]

A more reliable account was recorded by an editor of the New York *Herald* who wrote that "By throwing life and enthusiasm into her big toe Mrs. Margaret Fox Kane produced loud spirit rappings in the Academy of Music last night and dealt a death blow to spiritualism, that huge world-wide fraud which she and her sisters founded in 1848." The great hall, he wrote, "was crowded and the wildest excitement prevailed at times." Hundreds of spiritualists who had come saw "the originator of their faith destroy it at one stroke." At times Margaret was "hissed fiercely." It was "a most remarkable and dramatic spectacle."

As the curtain on one side of the stage parted, wrote the editor, "There she stood, a black-robed sharp-faced widow working her big toe and solemnly declaring that it was in this way she created the excitement that has driven so many persons to suicide and insanity." After a moment Margaret put on her glasses and slowly began to read in a

---

[9] New York *World*, October 21, 1888.

[10] New York *World*, October 22, 1888; for another story of the incident see New York *Times*, October 22, 1888.

voice trembling with emotion. "That I have been mainly instrumental in perpetrating the fraud of spiritualism," she said, "you already know. It is the greatest sorrow of my life. I began the deception when I was too young to know right from wrong."

Having made her declaration Margaret began her demonstration. "There was a dead silence," wrote the *Herald*'s editor; "everybody in the hall knew they were looking upon the woman who is principally responsible for spiritualism. She stood upon a little pine table, with nothing on her feet but stockings. As she remained motionless, loud distinct rappings were heard, now in the flies, now behind the scenes, now in the gallery." It was clear that the woman possessed a "devil's gift in a kind of rapping ventriloquism" from which spiritualism had "sprung into life, and here was the same toe rapping it out of existence."

At this point, wrote the editor, Margaret became very excited. She clapped her hands, danced about and cried, "It's a fraud! Spiritualism is a fraud from beginning to end! It's all a trick. There's no truth in it." As she finished her dancing-declaration "a whirlwind of applause followed." [11]

This demonstration attracted attention far and wide. Letters poured into the offices of the *World* begging further facts. Other mediums said that if Margaret had been a pure fraud it was well that the truth had been revealed; in any case, Margaret's evil doings did not prove that respectable spiritualist mediums were likewise frauds. It was clear to the members of spiritualist circles that the poor Fox girls had become hopeless alcoholics. If it had not been for the damage they had done they might well have been mere objects for pity.

For a while, after her appearance at the Academy of Music, Margaret lived a little better, using the money she had received from the *World* for the exposé and from lecture fees she earned on tours demonstrating the fraud she had previously practiced for so many years. But public interest in the "exposé sittings" soon disappeared entirely. Faced with stark necessity and the ever urgent need to buy wine, Margaret was reduced at length to the ignoble act of denying her confession and once more presiding at table séances as of old. At that time Dr. Funk,

[11] New York *Herald,* October 22, 1888.

a man unfriendly toward Margaret, wrote that "this unfortunate woman had sunk so low that for five dollars she would have denied her own mother and sworn to anything." [12]

It was amid these unhappy and degrading circumstances that finally, on March 8, 1893 Margaret Fox was seized with a fatal heart attack. Her earthly spirit left the mortal world in the home of her old friend, Mrs. Emily B. Ruggles, at 492 State Street in Brooklyn. Titus Merritt, the mortician at whose establishment she had often spent long nights sitting among the corpses watching for some sign of spirit-life, arranged the details for her burial at his well known funeral parlor in New York City. She had lived a long life. Yet, except for the few short months when Margaret had been associated with Doctor Elisha Kent Kane, her existence had been one of sorrow, anxiety, and shame. She always averred that she "never fully believed the rappings the work of spirits, but imagined some occult laws of nature concerned." [13] That she possessed remarkable insight—or clairvoyant talents—does not seem to be unlikely. Perhaps the tragedy of Margaret Fox lies in the fact that her extraordinary mental gifts were squandered merely to let loose one of the most amazing social phenomena of modern times.

[12] New York *Weekly Press*, November 20, 1889.

[13] Harry Houdini, *A Magician among the Spirits*, p. 11; see also Franklin Wesley Clark, "The Origins of Spiritualism in America," pp. 63–73, ms.

BIBLIOGRAPHY

Manuscripts

Anna Meister v. *Pennsylvania.* Unreported Cases of the Justice Court of Philadelphia, 1856. Justice Hall [City Hall], Philadelphia, Pennsylvania.

Ballinger, William Pitt. Diary. Rosenberg Library, Galveston, Texas.

British Consulate Papers. British Public Records Office, London, England.

Clark, Franklin Wesley. "The Origins of Spiritualism in America." Unpublished Master's thesis, University of Rochester, 1932. This is a very valuable paper on the origins of the cult in America.

Greeley, Horace. Papers. Folio–July, 1860. Library of Congress, Washington, D. C.

Newburyport School Board, 1873, Minutes of the. Newburyport School Board, Newburyport, Massachusetts, and New York Public Library, New York City, New York.

New York City "Coroner's Reports," December 5, 1856 (No. 1089). Department of Public Records, New York City, New York.

New York City School Board, 1879, Minutes of the. Department of Education, General Offices, New York City, New York.

Orphan's Court, 1865, Records of the. Unreported Cases Files No. 1072. Philadelphia, Pennsylvania.

Spirit-Love Society v. *City of New York.* Unreported Cases of Judge Henry Osborn's Court for October, 1855. Foley Square Court House Files, New York City, New York.

Spiritualism Collection. Folio 21. Philadelphia Public Library, Philadelphia, Pennsylvania.

United States v. *Hicks.* Unreported Cases for 1859 and 1860. United States Federal Court, New York City, New York.

Wakeman, Rhoda. "Deposition of Rhoda Wakeman." Unreported Cases for 1855–1856. District Court Records, New Haven, Connecticut.

Wakeman v. *Connecticut.* Unreported Cases for 1855–1856. District Court Records, New Haven, Connecticut.

Newspapers

Baltimore *Sun* (Maryland), 1857.
Boston *Courier* (Massachusetts), 1857.
Boston *Gazette* (Massachusetts), 1863.
Boston *Herald* (Massachusetts), 1872.
Boston *New Era* (Massachusetts), 1854.
Buffalo Commercial Advertizer (New York), 1851, 1854.
Buffalo *Courier* (New York), 1865.
Buffalo *Courier and Inquirer* (New York), 1850.
Buffalo *Express* (New York), 1865.
Charleston *Daily Courier* (South Carolina), 1868.
Galveston *Civilian* (Texas), 1857–1858.
Houston *Telegraph* (Texas), 1857.
Leavenworth *Times* (Kansas), 1879.
New Haven *Journal and Courier* (Connecticut), 1855.
New York *Evening Post* (New York), 1855, 1860.
New York *Herald* (New York), 1888.
New York *Journal of Commerce* (New York), 1850–1851.
New York *Times* (New York), 1852–1857, 1860, 1865–1866, 1868–1869,
    1872–1875, 1879–1881, 1885–1886, 1888.
New York *Tribune* (New York), 1849–1860, 1865, 1879.
New York *Weekly Press* (New York), 1889.
New York *World* (New York), 1888.
Philadelphia *Inquirer* (Pennsylvania), 1856, 1874.
Philadelphia *Pennsylvanian* (Pennsylvania), 1855.
Philadelphia *Press* (Pennsylvania), 1874.
Philadelphia *Public Ledger* (Pennsylvania), 1850, 1858, 1865.
Philadelphia *Telegraph* (Pennsylvania), 1865.
Providence *Journal* (Rhode Island), 1851, 1878.
Rochester *Democrat* (New York), 1848.
Rochester Magnet (New York), 1850.
Rochester *Union* (New York), 1886.
Times of London, 1854.
Washington *National Intelligencer* (D.C.), 1854.

Journal Articles

"Among the Materializers," *Nation*, XXXVIII (January 3, 1884), 9–10.
Congressional Globe, Thirty-First Congress, 1st Session, XXI, Part I, 644,

684, 884–891; Thirty-Third Congress, 1st Session, XXVIII, Part II, 923–924, 1082.

Cronise, Adelbert. "The Beginning of Modern Spiritualism in and near Rochester," *Rochester Historical Society, Publication Fund Series,* V (1926), 1–22.

"Demonology at Home and Abroad," *Blackwood's Magazine,* XCIX (April, 1866), 502–518.

"Discovery of the Source of the Rochester Knockings," *Buffalo Medical Journal,* VI (March, 1851), 628–642.

Edmonds, John Worth. "Judge Edmonds on 'Spiritualism'," *Nation,* I (September 7, 1865), 295–296.

"Free Love System, The" *Littell's Living Age,* 2d Series, X (September, 1855), 815–821.

James, Henry. "Modern Diabolism," *Atlantic Monthly,* XXXII (August, 1873), 219–224. A book review of *Modern Diabolism* by M. J. Williamson.

Journal of the American Society for Psychical Research, 1907–present.

Journal of the Society for Psychical Research (London), 1884–present.

Lippitt, F. J. "Was It Katie King?" *Galaxy,* XVIII (December, 1874), 754–766.

Owen, Robert Dale. "How I Came to Study Spiritual Phenomena," *Atlantic Monthly,* XXXIV (November, 1874), 578–590.

—. "Some Results from My Spiritual Studies," *Atlantic Monthly,* XXXIV (December, 1874), 719–731.

Perrone, F. "Spiritism and Modern Devilworship," *Dublin Review,* LXI (October, 1867), 253–280.

Proceedings of the American Society for Psychical Research, 1884–1889; New Series, 1907–present.

"Register of Students in William and Mary College, 1827–1881," *William and Mary Quarterly Historical Review,* 2d Series, IV (January, 1924), 131–136.

Spicer, Henry. "Spiritual Manifestations," *Littell's Living Age,* 2d Series, I (June, 1853), 807–820.

Books

Abbott, Lyman. *Henry Ward Beecher.* Boston & New York: Houghton, Mifflin and Company, 1903.

Barnum, P. T. *The Humbugs of The World.* New York: Carleton, 1866.

Bliss, Sylvester. *Memoir of William Miller.* Boston: J. V. Himes, 1853.

Boston *Courier. Spiritualism Shown As It Is! Boston Courier Report of Proceedings of Professed Spiritual Agents and Mediums in the Presence of Professors Pierce, Agassiz . . . and Others.* Boston: Boston *Courier:* 1857.

Branch, E. Douglas. *The Sentimental Years: 1836–1860.* New York: D. Appleton-Century Co., 1934.

Cadwaller, Mary E. *Hydesville in History.* Chicago: Progressive Thinker Publishing House, 1917.

Campbell, J. B., M.D. *Spiritualism.* New York: n.p., 1851. Pamphlet.

Capron, Eliab Wilkinson. *Modern Spiritualism: Its Facts and Fanaticisms, Its Consistencies and Contradictions.* Boston: B. Marsh, 1855; New York: Partridge and Brittan, 1855.

— and Henry D. Baron. *Singular Revelations . . . Noises in Western New York . . .* Auburn, New York: Finn and Rockwell, 1850.

Carmer, Carl. *Listen For a Lonesome Drum.* New York: Farrar and Rinehart, Inc., 1936.

Carrington, Hereword. *The Story of Psychic Science.* New York: Ives Washburn, 1931.

Clemens, Samuel L. [Mark Twain]. *The Washoe Giant in San Francisco.* Ed. with an introduction by Franklin Walker. San Francisco: G. Fields, 1938. Originally published in the *Golden Era* in the 1860's.

Davenport, Reuben Briggs. *The Death-Blow to Spiritualism: Being the True Story of the Fox Sisters As Revealed by the Authority of Margaret Fox Kane and Katherine Fox Jencken.* New York: Dillingham, 1888.

Davis, Andrew Jackson. *The Magic Staff: An Autobiography.* New York: J. S. Brown, 1857; Boston: B. Marsh, 1857.

—. *The Principles of Nature: Her Divine Revelations and a Voice to Mankind.* New York: S. S. Lyon and W. Fishbough, 1847.

—. *The Philosophy of Spiritual Intercourse: Being an Explanation of Modern Mysteries.* New York: Fowlers and Wells, 1856.

de Rothschild, Solomon A. *Casual View of America: The Home Letters of Solomon de Rothschild, 1859–1861.* Stanford, California: Stanford University Press, 1961.

Dewey, D. M. *History of the Strange Sounds or Rappings.* New York: D. M. Dewey, 1850.

Dixon, William Hepworth. *New America.* 2 vols. London: Hurst and Blackett, 1867.

Doyle, Arthur Conan. *The History of Spiritualism.* London, New York, etc.: Cassell and Co., Ltd., 1926; New York: George H. Doran Company, 1926.

Edmonds, John Worth and George T. Dexter. *Spiritualism*. New York: Partridge and Brittan, 1854.

Elder, William. *Biography of Elisha Kent Kane*. Philadelphia: Childs and Peterson, 1858.

Fauset, Arthur Huff. *Sojourner Truth: God's Faithful Pilgrim*. In "Chapel Hill Series of Negro Biographies," ed. by Benjamin Brawley. Chapel Hill: The University of North Carolina Press, 1938.

[Fox, Margaret]. *Memoir and the Love-Life of Doctor Kane: Containing the Correspondence, and a History of the Acquaintance, Engagement and Secret Marriage between Elisha K. Kane and Margaret Fox*. New York: Carleton, 1866.

Garland, Hamlin. *Forty Years of Psychic Research*. New York: Macmillan Company, 1936.

Goodrich-Freer, A. *Essays in Psychical Research*. London: G. Redway, 1899.

Gordon, William Robert. *Threefold Test of Modern Spiritualism*. New York: C. Scribner, 1856.

Grattan, Thomas Colley. *Civilized America*. 2 vols. London: Bradbury and Evans, 1859.

Greeley, Horace. *Recollections of a Busy Life*. New York: J. B. Ford and Company, 1868.

Hale, William Harlan. *Horace Greeley: Voice of The People*. New York: Harper & Brothers, 1950.

Hall, Courtney R. "Henry Seybert," in *Dictionary of American Biography,* XVII, 3, New York: Charles Scribner's Sons, 1935. This volume edited by Dumas Malone; the whole work is jointly edited by Allen Johnson and Dumas Malone.

Hammond, Charles. *Light from The Spirit World* . . . Rochester: Dewey, 1852.

Hardinge, Emma. *Modern American Spiritualism: A Twenty Years' Record of the Communication between Earth and the World of Spirits*. New York: Emma Hardinge, 1870.

Hare, Robert. *Experimental Investigation of Spirit Manifestations: Demonstrating the Existence of Spirits and Their Communication with Mortals*. New York: Partridge and Brittan, 1856.

Hertzler, J. O. *The History of Utopian Thought*. New York: Macmillan Company, 1923.

Home, Daniel Douglas. *Lights and Shadows of Spiritualism.* New York: G. W. Carleton & Co., 1879.

Houdini, Harry. *A Magician among the Spirits.* New York: Harper & Brothers, 1924.

Howitt, William. *The History of The Supernatural In All Ages and Nations and in all Churches Christian and Pagan: Demonstrating A Universal Faith.* London: Longman's, 1863.

James, William. *The Letters of William James.* 2 vols. Edited by his son, Henry James. Boston: *Atlantic Monthly* Press, 1920.

—. *William James on Psychical Research.* Compiled and edited by Gardner Murphy and Robert Ballou. New York: The Viking Press, 1960.

Johnson, Allen, and Dumas Malone (ed.). *Dictionary of American Biography.* 22 vols. New York: Charles Scribner's Sons, 1928–1937.

Kane, Elisha Kent, M.D. U.S.N. *The United States Grinnell Expedition in Search of Sir John Franklin: A Personal Narrative.* New York: The Viking Press, 1960.

King-Hall, Magdalen. *The Fox Sisters: a Novel.* London: P. Davies, 1950.

Leopold, Richard W. *Robert Dale Owen: A Biography,* in "Harvard Historical Studies," Vol. XLV. Cambridge: Harvard University Press, 1940.

Lincoln, Abraham. *The Collected Works of Abraham Lincoln.* 9 vols. Edited by Roy P. Basler. New Brunswick, New Jersey: Rutgers University Press, 1953–1955.

Maynard, Nettie Colburn. *Was Abraham Lincoln a Spiritualist?* London: Spiritualist Press, 1917. Written in 1891, published in 1917.

National Laboratory of Psychical Research. *Short Title Catalog of Works on Psychical Research, Spiritualism, Magic, Psychology, Legerdemain and Other Methods of Deception, Charlatanism, Witchcraft, and Technical Works from Circa 1450 A.D. to 1929 A.D.* Compiled by Harry Price. London: National Laboratory of Psychical Research, 1929.

Nevins, Allan and Milton Halsey Thomas (eds.) *The Diary of George Templeton Strong.* 2 vols. New York: The Macmillan Company, 1952.

Nye, Russel Blaine. *George Bancroft: Brahmin Rebel.* New York: Alfred A. Knopf, 1944.

Owen, Robert Dale. *The Debatable Land between This World and The Next.* New York: Carleton, 1872.

. *Footfalls on The Boundary of Another World.* Philadelphia: Lippincott, 1860.

Pennsylvania University. *Seybert Commission for Investigating Modern Spiritualism. Preliminary Report of the Commission Appointed by the*

University of Pennsylvania to Investigate Modern Spiritualism in Accordance with the Request of the Late Henry Seybert. Philadelphia: Lippincott, 1887.

Perry, Ralph Barton. *The Thought and Character of William James.* Boston: Little, Brown, 1935.

Podmore, Frank. *Modern Spiritualism: A History and a Criticism.* 2 vols. London: Methuen, 1902.

Pond, Mariam Buckner. *Time Is Kind: the Story of the Unfortunate Fox Family.* New York: Centennial Press, 1947. This was published simultaneously in England under the title, *The Unwilling Martyrs.* Originally, it was issued in mimeographed form under the title, *The Unfortunate Fox Family.*

Porter, Katherine H. *Through A Glass Darkly: Spiritualism in the Browning Circle.* Lawrence, Kansas: University of Kansas Press, 1958.

Rochester Knockings! Discovery and Explanation of the Source of the Phenomena Generally Known as the Rochester Knockings. Buffalo: G. H. Derby, 1851.

Sandburg, Carl. *Abraham Lincoln: The War Years.* 4 vols. New York: Harcourt, Brace, 1939.

Seldes, Gilbert. *The Stammering Century.* New York: John Day Co., 1927.

Smith, (Mrs.) E. Vale. *History of Newburyport.* Boston: Press of Damrell and Moore, 1854.

Smith, Timothy L. *Revivalism and Social Reform in Mid-Nineteenth Century America.* New York: Abingdon Press, 1957.

Smucker, Samuel M. [Schmucker, Samuel M.]. *The Life of Dr. Elisha Kent Kane.* Philadelphia: J. W. Bradley, 1860.

Spicer, Henry. *Sights and Sounds: The Mystery of the Day, Comprising an Entire History of the American "Spirit" Manifestations.* London: T. Bosworth, 1853.

Strong, George Templeton. *See* Nevins, Allan.

Taylor, Mrs. Sarah Elizabeth Langworthy (ed.). *Fox-Taylor Automatic Writing, 1869–1892: Unabridged Record.* Minneapolis, Minnesota: Tribune-Great West Printing Company, 1932.

Taylor, W. G. Langworthy. *Katie Fox: Epochmaking Medium and the Making of the Fox-Taylor Record.* New York: G. P. Putnam's Sons, 1933.

Thurston, Herbert. *Modern Spiritualism.* London: Sheed and Ward, 1928.

Tyler, Alice Felt. *Freedom's Ferment.* Minneapolis: The University of Minnesota Press, 1944.

Underhill, Ann Leah [Fox]. *The Missing Link in Modern Spiritualism.* New York: T. R. Knox and Co., 1885.

Walz, Jay and Audrey. *Undiscovered Country.* New York: Duell, Sloan and Pearce, Inc., 1958.

White, Stewart Edward. *The Stars Are Still There.* New York: E. P. Dutton & Co., Inc., 1946.

Wilson, Forrest. *Crusader in Crinoline: The Life of Harriet Beecher Stowe.* Philadelphia: J. B. Lippincott Co., 1941.

INDEX